Will Shortz presents
the Puzzle Doctor:

KENKEN® FEVER

"KenKen®: Logic Puzzles That Make You Smarter":

Will Shortz Presents KenKen Easiest, Volume 1
Will Shortz Presents KenKen Easy, Volume 2
Will Shortz Presents KenKen Easy to Hard, Volume 3
Will Shortz Presents The Little Gift Book of KenKen
Will Shortz Presents Crazy for KenKen Easiest
Will Shortz Presents Crazy for KenKen Easy
Will Shortz Presents Crazy for KenKen Easy to Hard
Will Shortz Presents KenKen for the Seaside
Will Shortz Presents KenKen for Your Coffee Break
Will Shortz Presents KenKen for Stress Relief
Will Shortz Presents Tame KenKen
Will Shortz Presents Wild KenKen
Will Shortz Presents Ferocious KenKen
Will Shortz Presents the Ultimate KenKen Omnibus

KenKen for Kids

Will Shortz Presents I Can KenKen! Volume 1
Will Shortz Presents I Can KenKen! Volume 2
Will Shortz Presents I Can KenKen! Volume 3

WILL SHORTZ PRESENTS
THE PUZZLE DOCTOR:
KENKEN®
FEVER

150 EASY TO HARD LOGIC PUZZLES THAT MAKE YOU SMARTER

TETSUYA MIYAMOTO

INTRODUCTION BY
WILL SHORTZ

ST. MARTIN'S GRIFFIN
NEW YORK

www.stmartins.com

ISBN 978-0-312-64111-5

First Edition: May 2010

10 9 8 7 6 5 4 3 2 1

Introduction

If you consider all the world's greatest puzzle varieties, the ones that have inspired crazes over the years—crosswords, jigsaw puzzles, tangrams, sudoku, etc.—they have several properties in common. They . . .

- Are simple to learn
- Have great depth
- Are variable in difficulty, from easy to hard
- Are mentally soothing and pleasing
- Have some unique feature that makes them different from everything else and instantly addictive

By these standards, a new puzzle called KenKen, the subject of the book you're holding, has the potential to become one of the world's greats.

KenKen is Japanese for "square wisdom" or "cleverness squared."

The rules are simple: Fill the grid with digits so as not to repeat a digit in any row or column (as in sudoku) and so the digits within each heavily outlined group of boxes combine to make the arithmetic result indicated.

The simplest KenKen puzzles start with 3×3 boxes and use only addition. Harder examples have larger grids and more arithmetic operations.

KenKen was invented in 2003 by Tetsuya Miyamoto, a Japanese math instructor, as a means to help his students learn arithmetic and develop logical thinking. Tetsuya's education method is unusual. Put simply, he doesn't teach. His philosophy is to make the tools of learning available to students and then let them progress on their own.

Tetsuya's most popular learning tool has been KenKen, which his students spend hours doing and find more engaging than TV and video games.

It's true that KenKen has great capacity for educating and building the mind. But first and foremost it's a puzzle to be enjoyed. It is to numbers what the crossword puzzle is to words.

So turn the page and begin. . . .

—Will Shortz

How to Solve KenKen

KenKen is a logic puzzle with simple rules:

- Fill the grid with digits so as not to repeat a digit in any row or column.
- Digits within each heavily outlined group of squares, called a cage, must combine to make the arithmetic result indicated.
- A 3×3–square puzzle will use the digits from 1 to 3, a 4×4–square puzzle will use the digits from 1 to 4, etc.

Solving a KenKen puzzle involves pure logic and mathematics. No guesswork is needed. Every puzzle has a unique solution.

In this volume of KenKen, the puzzles use all four arithmetic operations—addition, subtraction, multiplication, and division—in the following manner:

- In a cage marked with a plus sign, the given number will be the sum of the digits you enter in the squares.
- In a cage marked with a minus sign, the given number will be the difference between the digits you enter in the squares (the lower digit subtracted from the higher one).
- In a cage marked with a multiplication sign, the given number will be the product of the digits you enter in the squares.
- In a cage marked with a division sign, the given number will be the quotient of the digits you enter in the squares.

Take the 5×5–square example on this page.

48×		3+		4−
	8+	10×	4+	
3−				2÷
	4+		4	
7+			15×	

To start, fill in any digits in 1×1 sections—in this puzzle, the 4 in the fourth row. These are literally no-brainers.

Next, look for sections whose given numbers are either high or low, or that involve distinctive combinations of digits, since these are often the easiest to solve. For example, the L-shaped group in the upper left has a product of 48. The only combination of three digits from 1 to 5 that multiplies to 48 is 3, 4, and 4. Since the two 4s can't appear in the same row or column, they must appear at the ends of the L. The 3 goes between them.

Now look at the pair of squares in the first row with a sum of 3. The only two digits that add up to 3 are 1 and 2. We don't know their order yet, but this information can still be useful.

Sometimes, the next step in solving a KenKen puzzle is to ignore the given numbers and use sudoku-like logic to avoid repeating a digit in a row or column. For example, now that 1, 2, 3, and 4 have been used or are slated for use in the first row, the remaining square (at the end of the row) must be a 5. Then the digit below the 5 must be a 1 for this pair of squares to have a difference of 4.

Next, consider the pair of squares in the third column with a product of 10. The only two digits from 1 to 5 that have a product of 10 are 2 and 5. We don't know their order yet. However, the digit in the square above them, which we previously identified as either a 1 or a 2, must be 1, so as not to repeat a 2 in this column. The 2 that accompanies the 1 goes to its right.

Continuing in this way, using these and other techniques left for you to discover, you can work your way around the grid, filling in the rest of the squares. The complete solution is shown on the following page.

48× 3	4	**3+** 1	2	**4−** 5
4	**8+** 5	**10×** 2	**4+** 3	1
3− 2	3	5	1	**2÷** 4
5	**4+** 1	3	**4** 4	2
7+ 1	2	4	**15×** 5	3

Additional Tips

- In advanced KenKen puzzles, as you've seen, cages can have more than two squares. It's okay for a cage to repeat a digit—as long as the digit is not repeated in a row or column.
- Cages with more than two squares will always involve addition or multiplication. Subtraction and division occur only in cages with exactly two squares.
- Remember, in doing KenKen, you never have to guess. Every puzzle can be solved by using step-by-step logic. Keep going, and soon you'll be a KenKen master!

Light and Easy +/−/×/÷ 1

5−	4−		32×		8+
	2÷			3÷	
5+		8+			3÷
1−		3−		15×	
3−	2−		6		5+
	11+		3÷		

3÷		24×		7+	
2−	5−	6+		8×	24×
		8+	2		
240×			11+		45×
		3÷			
	8×		3÷		

Light and Easy +/−/×/÷ 3

5−		3	40×		
10+	5+	11+		5+	12+
		2÷			
30×	3÷		11+		
		2÷		5−	
3−		2÷		5+	

4 Light and Easy +/−/×/÷

90×	3+		10+		15+
	3÷		7+		
		2÷	1−	3+	
160×					3+
	2−		8+		
	7+		5−		3

Light and Easy +/−/×/÷   **5**

6+		**3−**		**48×**	
1−		**60×**	**3+**		
2÷			**11+**	**9×**	
	60×				**1**
3+			**480×**		
3−		**2÷**		**5**	

60×	18×			4	3÷
	2÷		4−	3+	
	11+				15×
5−	2÷		2÷	2÷	
	2−				20×
1−		24×			

4−	2÷	5−	2÷	1−	
				20×	
7+	6×			11+	5−
	11+				
3÷	4−	1−	3−	2÷	
				3÷	

8 Light and Easy +/−/×/÷

5+		11+		6×	
2−	5−	11+		30×	2÷
		2			
24×	2−		3+		20×
	20×	3÷	5−	13+	

Light and Easy +/−/×/÷

3+	12×		6+		3−
	17+				
2÷		3−	3÷	1−	
1−	11+			3÷	3−
		8×			
6+			6	5+	

1−		3÷		2−	5+
2÷	10×				
	5−	7+			11+
3+		12+			
	9+		3	3÷	5+
1−		5−			

Light and Easy +/−/×/÷ 11

3	**11+**		**48×**	**2÷**	
5−				**8+**	
20×		**5+**	**3÷**		
1−			**15×**		**2−**
4×		**11+**			
	7+		**5**	**1−**	

2÷	18×			7+	
	11+	10+		6+	
5−				2÷	1−
	15+		2		
75×		2−		2÷	
		2÷		5−	

Light and Easy +/−/×/÷ 13

2÷	24×		3−		90×
		1−	2÷	3÷	
2÷					
12+	2÷		4−		8×
	3−		10+		
	3+		3−		

4	1−		6×		
3+		2÷	3−	60×	
15+					5−
	2÷		13+		
30×	3	5+	5−		40×

Light and Easy +/−/×/÷ 15

6	3÷		3−		1−
3+		40×	2−		
2−				5−	
2−		120×		3÷	
72×			3+		10×
	4−		2÷		

3÷	20×	1−		10+	
		30×	5+		
10+				1−	3÷
3−		2÷	15×		
3	3×			3÷	1−
		2−			

2÷	15+	12×	60×	2÷	
		•			1
360×		3−		5+	
	6×	3÷		1−	
		1−	15×		
				2÷	

40×			10+		
4−		13+	12×	2÷	
11+					7+
	3+		2−		
12×	5−		2−		11+
	5+		4−		

Moderate +/−/×/÷   19

5	4−		3÷		120×
15+		5+	3÷		
				2÷	
3÷		11+	1−	3÷	
8×				60×	
	3÷		1−		

6+		2÷		2÷	
5−	24×	360×			
			5+	1−	2÷
1−	3−				
	3−		20×		
24×		3÷		3−	

Moderate +/−/×/÷ 21

50×	2÷		5−		8+
		3−			
2−		1	20×	1−	
5−	1−	60×		2÷	11+
3÷		3÷		1−	

24×	1−	4−	2÷		1−
			3+		
1−		20×		48×	
2−		5−			
2÷	5−	1−	20×		11+
			7+		

360×		2÷	5−		1−
			15×		
9+		1−	3÷	1−	
3+				2−	
3	9+	3÷	10+		20×
			3−		

5−	60×	2÷		1	7+
			2÷		
1−	1−		2÷		72×
	2÷		7+		
3	18×		12+		
2÷				7+	

2÷		1−		1−	
12×			72×	15×	
15×				16×	
15+					
7+	1−			18×	6
		20×			

6×	1−	6+		2−	
		10+			3−
15+			5+		
11+			5+		2−
3−	2÷	15+			
		1−		11+	

3−		36×		12×	9+
24×					
2÷		3+		2−	
	10+	3−		4−	
		90×	120×		2÷
1−					

4−		15×		1−	
1−	3÷				4−
	12+	1−		12+	
		5−			
1	13+		14+		36×
3+					

36×	3÷		1−		13+
		4−	2÷		
96×				8+	
	3−		5−		
3+		1−		1−	
8+		2−		1−	

4	11+		3÷		60×
5−	11+			3	
	1−		2÷		
60×	10+		3−		12×
		11+			
	3÷		11+		

24×	6×			1−	
	3÷	5	30×		12×
		3−		24×	
30×	10+		12×		4−
	15+			2÷	

3÷	1−		5−		20×
	4−		1−		
4−	2÷		7+		3÷
	9+	2÷	3−	2−	
7+					3÷
	4−		4−		

15×		10+	32×	1−	
120×					10+
		3−			
2÷	2÷	3÷		1−	3−
		3−			
2÷		1−		1−	

1−	15×			12+	24×
	60×				
2−		3÷	6+		
1−				9+	
2−	2−			10+	
	3	3−			

Challenging +/−/×/÷

40×		10+	2÷	9+	
	13+			6	
1−			4	1−	2÷
		6×			
3÷		11+		2−	
2÷		9+		2÷	

2−		10+		360×	1−
12×					
	1−		9+		5−
	8+				
6		48×	9+		3−
3÷					

60×	3÷		3÷		8+
		5−	15+		
9+				8+	
	18×	4		48×	
		2−	1−		
5+				30×	

15×		3−		15+	3÷
2−					
2÷	2−		3−	6+	
	8+			2÷	
5−		120×			2−
1−		3÷			

Challenging +/−/×/÷

12×		8+	3÷	10+	
				9+	
1−	2−	5+			3−
		2−		12×	
1−	1−		1−		
	5+			3÷	

24×		1−		6+	
	1−		1−		
8+		1−		50×	
	18+	2÷		108×	
		12+	7+		

4−	24×		1−		2÷
	2−		2−		
2÷		2−		5−	
1−		3−		1−	
1−	5−	2÷		1−	9+
		3÷			

30×		1−	20×	3÷	
				1−	
15+			1−		6+
24×			6×		
20×		5−	3÷	2−	
	3			20×	

Challenging +/−/×/÷ 43

4−		**1−**		**2−**	
5+	**9+**		**1−**	**20×**	
		30×		**6+**	**5**
1−	**7+**		**6×**		
				2÷	
3−		**9+**		**2÷**	

36×	5	6+			40×
		2÷	3−	2−	
6+					
3÷		1−	1−	1−	15+
48×					
		2÷			

3÷		20×		3÷	
14+		5−	7+	9+	
9+					2÷
	72×				
2÷		2÷		1−	
3−		1−		1−	

72×	5−		8+	3	12+
	5				
	13+	8+	7+	2÷	
14+				2÷	
		9+		1−	
				1−	

5	3−		12×		12+
3−	3÷	8+			
		2−		2÷	
2÷	12×		18×		1
				60×	3÷
30×					

60×			2÷		5−
11+		2÷		6+	
3÷		2−			12×
	18×	4−		7+	
		1−			3−
3	5+		4−		

Challenging +/−/×/÷ 49

2÷	2÷		1−		7+
	6+		24×		
3−		2−	6+	1−	
3÷				2−	
3−		8+	3÷	30×	
7+				1−	

16+	72×				7+
	2÷		30×		
		17+			
5−			10×		14+
24×				48×	

Light and Easy +/−/×/÷   51

13+		40×		9+		
2÷			252×		3	35×
2÷	11+			6−		
		3÷		2−		
60×		14×			144×	
	6−		30×			
6−		72×			10×	

52 Light and Easy +/−/×/÷

105×		2÷		6−		5−
	14+	11+			300×	
24×			3÷			11+
		6−				
5−		12+			14×	
7+	6−		2	72×		15×
	1	168×				

2−		6−		90×		
15×			168×	13+		16+
3÷	3÷	30×				
			6×	32×		
5	1176×					5−
			210×	30×		
1−					1−	

6−		12×		3−		2−
12×	10×		14×		2÷	
		12+				14+
28×		3÷		3×		
30×	3	13+			28×	
	3+		1−			3÷
3÷		4	15+			

Light and Easy +/−/×/÷ 55

1−	13+		1−	6×		
	2÷	5+		1−	3−	7+
5			6−			
3÷	14×			1−		5
	8+	30×	3	2÷	5−	8+
6−			2÷			
	7+			210×		

56 Light and Easy +/−/×/÷

20×		144×		6−	3÷	
10+		15×			2−	7
			4−			10×
13+		1−		5+		
14+	1	6−	2÷		60×	
	2÷		4×	1−		
					28×	

7+	13+	3÷		3÷	35×	
		120×			6×	
2÷			13+	15×		24×
3−		6−			120×	
7+			9+			
5−	2−			3−		6
		3−			6−	

90×			2÷		3−	
1−	2÷		18+			14+
	21×	4	6−		2÷	
		11+				
14×		60×			5−	
120×			3−	3	6−	
1	13+			24×		

2÷		24×	11+	2÷		13+
4−				6−	5	
120×	14+				3+	60×
			3÷			
	6×		13+	60×		
3	42×				112×	2÷
		2−				

60 Light and Easy +/−/×/÷

18+	84×			20×	1−	
	3+	10×	5−		14+	2÷
24×		6−	2÷		8+	
6×	1−		1−	18+		5−
		14+		3÷		
	7				5+	

Light and Easy +/−/×/÷   61

525×			4−	2÷		11+
3+		17+		13+		
	12+				20×	
15×			3−			9+
	2	12+				
288×			6−	105×		
	5+			10+		

1−	1−		5−		1−	3+
	4−	5−	105×			
6−				13+	4	210×
	3+		4		5+	
17+		1−	8+			
3÷					8+	7+
	10+		7+			

21×	2	24×			10+	
	6−		15+			
3÷	10+		6−		6×	1−
		14+				
20×	3÷		5+	4−		8+
	12+			13+		
3÷			3÷		11+	

13+		105×	56×			19+
40×				60×		
	105×					
		4	144×	3+		11+
2÷		3+				
	13+		150×	21×		3−

Light and Easy +/−/×/÷   65

12×	5	3÷		13+		13+
		3÷	10+			
1−			7		5−	
3÷	6−	84×			1−	20×
		240×		6−		
21×	3÷				1−	3÷
		20×				

2÷	300×		6−		2÷	
	4			15+	120×	4−
294×	3÷					
		2	8+			3−
15×	1−		2	10+		
	20+					84×
			1−			

3÷		72×	35×	28×	4−	
8+						13+
		15+				
13+		2		20×		
20×	12+			13+		10+
		21×				
4−		8+			10+	

30×		42×	10+	2÷	14×	
6−						1−
	7+			10+		
12×			36×	16+		
4−		11+		10+	11+	
15+						6+
		6−		5		

Moderate +/−/×/÷   69

6−		13+	1−	2÷		20×
3−	5+			75×		
		7+	13+		2÷	4−
2−				2		
2÷	3−			28×	2−	
		2−	2−			6−
3−				13+		

70 Moderate +/−/×/÷

2÷	72×	1−		70×		10×
			1−		6−	
17+	4−			13+		
		9+			2÷	
	6−		3+		1−	168×
4−	2−	6		20×		
		2−				

Moderate +/−/×/÷ 71

1−	40×	13+		16+		3−
			30×			
6−	1−			3÷		2−
	4−		2−	5+		
84×				2−	3÷	
11+			2÷		5−	
5	6−			13+		

6−	2÷		1−		2−	
	40×			2÷		8+
13+	1	14+	12×	2−		
	2÷			4	3−	
				3−		2÷
12×	18+			2÷		
	5+		4−		1−	

3+	1−	126×			60×	1−
		6−				
2−	3+	12+			2−	7+
		3	5−			
13+	3−		30×	4−		12+
	3÷			6−		
	4−		2	1−		

74 Moderate +/−/×/÷

6−	13+		4−	2−	10+	6×
	6+					
		2−		105×		17+
16+		6−	2÷		2	
	12×				16+	
672×			1−	1−		6+

2−	35×	3+		3	13+	2−
		12+		3+		
24×			7		30×	
6−		2÷	3−	35×		1−
	14+				35×	
		12+				
1−		210×			3−	

76 Moderate +/−/×/÷

24×	11+		1−		1−	
			2÷	1−		840×
36×	252×	7				
			5	2÷	3−	
		168×			60×	
6−		80×		2−		
			2÷		6−	

2−	2−		90×		8×	
	1−					
13+			14+	2÷		10+
10+		5		6−		
6+				1−		
3÷	2÷		1008×			14+
	12+					

5−	20×			3÷		2÷
	16+		3−		42×	
24×		22+		3		
	2÷			18+	1−	
	6×				13+	
2−			3−			4−
	3÷			3−		

3÷	140×		2÷		2÷	2÷
		25+				
11+	6×	2−			10+	5+
			6−			
12+				15+		
28×	4−		2÷	2−		5−
	1−			4−		

4−	3÷	12+	5−		30×	3−
30×		1−		17+	6−	
1−		6−				3
6×		3−			1−	
3−	6−	3÷	5	84×		7+
			2÷			

Challenging +/−/×/÷   81

4−	3÷		24×		3−		6−
	2÷		15+	35×	4÷		
56×	24×				24×		
		1−			2÷	4÷	
35×			1−	3÷		7−	
2÷	1	23+			14×	60×	
	64×		7−			14+	
				1−			

4−		2÷	2−	6×	11+	21+	8
2−							24×
2−	18+				1−		
	7−		1−			10×	3÷
4−	2÷		4−		40×		
	14+					8+	70×
2÷		1−	1−	15+	2÷		
4−							

Challenging +/−/×/÷   83

26+	1−		56×	8×		6×	
	13+				16+	6+	7+
	10+		16+				
				2÷	3÷	21+	
24×	20×	6−					280×
		13+		21+			
			15×	15+			
	4÷					13+	

2−	42×		1−		4−	4÷	
		6+				3−	
7	15+			7−		10+	7+
5−			1−				
2−		18+	7+		32×	3÷	12+
16×			1				
	32×	280×			2−	3÷	
			8+			13+	

4÷	26+	105×	280×			3−	6×
			3÷	4−	13+		
1−						96×	2
		2−	1−				
42×	10+			105×		280×	
		11+	2−	1−			
13+						13+	1−
			13+				

3÷		35×	2÷		19+	1−	
2÷						6−	
17+		10+		2÷		15×	
	19+		2−		120×		
112×			2÷			10+	
	16+		16×	18+	7−		
13+					2÷	84×	
	2÷					4	

24×		1−	10×	4−	7+	3−	
35×	6−					4−	3÷
		2÷		16×			
2÷	3−		7−		1−		4−
	2−				15×		
2÷		1−	8+		14+	11+	
2−			2−			2÷	
5−		1−		2÷		4−	

2÷		14+		2÷		7−	
4÷	128×		2−		7	15+	3÷
			15+	2÷			
10×					168×		
15+		2÷		7−		48×	
	24×		2−	8+	120×		
3−	17+					48×	2−
			1−				

5−	24×		3−		18+		5−
		2÷	14+				
14+	4−				48×		60×
	26+	42×		224×		56×	
		40×			10+		
3−							2−
		56×	1−		2÷		
5−			24×			6+	

7−	160×		3÷	2−	17+		3÷
	10+					13+	
4−		6−		18+			1−
		6	26+	15+			
10+					24×	3−	
2−	4÷						4−
	2÷			16×	3−		
1−		11+				5−	

168×			6+			3−	14+
6−	17+	12×			4−		
			175×			1−	2÷
6×		11+		4−			
7+			24×	13+		2÷	2−
2÷	10+				4−		
		1−		192×		2−	11+
60×							

2÷		2−	3÷	16+		2÷	
3−				80×		1−	4−
7+	5−	7−					
		4−		5−	13+		
5−	4÷	20×			336×		
		4÷		12+		9+	1−
4−		3÷	24×		30×		
2−						2÷	

42×		3÷		21+	192×		
28×		13+	8+			3+	3−
12+							
6+			4÷		7−	13+	
	13+	168×	3−			20×	
			1−	5−		126×	
2÷				9+	19+		
2−		10×					

1−		1−		56×		7+	6−
30×		22+	1−		7−		
11+						4	13+
112×		13+	10+				
			5−		13+		2÷
9+		504×			15×		
4÷			1−			3−	2÷
4−		4−		4−			

Challenging +/−/×/÷ 95

336×			4÷		5−		4−
	21+	150×			15+		
		10+		24×		96×	
24+				4÷	14×		
		210×				2−	
288×			168×	2−		1−	
					1−		2÷
			5−		1−		

3+	21×	96×		108×			140×	6+
		432×						
24+			162×	8−		3÷		11+
24×				7	15×			
	3÷	4÷	120×			8×	25+	7
135×			11+					
		10+	3+		19+		5−	
40×			42×				2÷	
8−		112×			1−		2÷	

63×			18+			30×		
5−		140×			8−		3÷	
3+		48×	17+		35×	13+	12×	
13+			13+				1−	
12+		8+		5−	24×	36×	270×	
30×			3+					17+
	10+			6−		1−		
17+	10×		15+		18×			28×
	12×			3+		3−		

21×			24×		315×		4÷	2−
8−	30×		72×		17+			
		7	11+			12+	10+	8−
6	17+			9+				
2÷	8−	6−			3+		2−	
		1−				17+	24×	8+
15×	5−		3+		3−			
	9+		24×			15×	8−	48×
48×			16+					

Light and Easy +/−/×/÷ 99

2÷		21+	3+		28×		1−	
2÷	1−				8−		45×	5+
		3+	18+			40×		
432×	2÷		3−	13+			7+	140×
		735×		17+	5	54×		
	3÷						3÷	
35×		720×		5		126×		15+
			576×	3÷				
				9+				

100 Light and Easy +/−/×/÷

18+	3+		45×		10+		11+	2−
			17+		7−			
35×	17+	224×	3÷			2÷		6−
		9+		336×				
4		24×	3+		90×			
8−	3−	2÷				1400×		
	3÷		3÷		1−			
6−	8−	98×	3−			2÷	4÷	
	4−			2−				

3÷	2÷		1−		21×			40×
	6−		2÷		5−	3÷		
1−	2÷	8−	2÷			3−	7+	3÷
			18+					
3+	90×		16+			17+		3÷
		3÷		1−		36×		
2−		3−	48×			3÷	5−	
192×			9	5+			196×	
	17+		10×			2÷		

3+	2÷	42×			3−	360×		
		2÷		4−		5−	6−	6+
13+	2−	3÷			3+			
		45×		17+		18×	2÷	
	13+		3+		17+		4−	
12+	8−	4		7+			30×	
		3÷				6−	42×	3÷
1−	2÷	15+			4−			
		90×				28×		

Light and Easy +/−/×/÷

3÷		35×		8−		28+	10+	
8+	23+	3÷						19+
			135×			3+		
	144×		3+	30×	6−	11+		
35×	18+						270×	8−
		7	17+	24×	3÷	20×		
17+		2÷						60×
	7+		84×		4−		504×	
2								

104 Light and Easy +/−/×/÷

2÷	16×		4−		23+	14+		8−
	12+		8−	3−		6		
14+						168×		
	126×		2÷		3+		17+	
4÷			810×					2
11+	8−		7+		42×		720×	
	84×		2−	3+	8−			
128×		15+			140×		8+	12×
			6−					

50×		16×	3÷	2÷		36×		17+
			1−		17+			
63×	1−	35×		4÷			3÷	
		8−		14+	23+		5−	
54×		3				3+	2÷	
3÷	28×	5−		6			2−	
		14+		7−		8+	8+	
8	15+		4−	2−			15+	
2÷			3÷		5−			

13+	8−		3÷		4−		35×	
		14+		4−		210×	5−	4÷
6×		17+						
40×		14+	24×	42×		17+		6
				8		8−		3−
42×	17+			2÷		8+		
		13+	105×		6+		4÷	17+
360×					48×			
	2−		8−				2÷	

Light and Easy +/−/×/÷

4÷	756×		315×			4÷		19+
			8−	15+		16+		
20×		13+						
270×		5−		144×	5+		8+	
	112×	2÷			7	12+		
		4÷			8−		12×	
11+		5−		100×	108×	19+		6×
	8−							
	9+		48×			22+		

3÷		1−	168×		30×	8+	2÷	
20×	4÷			8−			50×	
		2÷			2−			1−
	8−		3+	128×		2÷		
18×	21×	2−		8		7+	3−	7+
			16+		18×			
2−		7−	7			3−	2÷	
13+			30×				36×	
3−		19+			3+		10+	

Light and Easy +/−/×/÷

18+	36×		9+	13+	8−	2÷		11+
						17+	8+	
112×	19+		7+					1−
		168×	5			8−		
2−			17+	6	2÷		6−	
16×			135×		54×			4÷
	15×				1008×		4÷	
20+		84×	28×					6−
	2÷				9+			

72×		3−		210×		2÷		27×
		8−	18+		15+			
48×					5−	30×		
17+	3+	5−	8−	7+		240×	1−	
					5		11+	
		48×		2	3+		5−	
11+		20×	18×			23+		
4−				20+	4−		10×	
17+		3−						

Moderate +/−/×/÷   111

12×		112×	12+			45360×	
40×						8−	
	15+		8−	12×		9+	
17+		13+		6×		1−	
63×	2−	3÷		1−	3+	24×	3÷
		16×		2688×			
3+	3÷		3÷			30×	13+
		158760×	120×				
2−						2−	

6	6×	315×	40×			90×	16+	24+
4÷			30+					
				54×				
1−	20×		420×		378×	6−		2÷
	288×					140×		
		2−				3+		
11+			8−		450×		2÷	
135×	20+							192×
		2÷		126×				

25×		24×		8+	24+			7−
	19+	1440×	2−			3÷	4	
			3−			6+	5−	
			17+	8−	108×	21×		
4÷	5−							5
	252×		120×			3−	56×	
2÷		8−			21+			
378×	3		14+				7+	
		2÷		18+				

4÷		80×		3−	17+		48×	
14+	2÷	3÷				7+	12×	8−
			240×					
	1−		15+	1	8−	13+		
45×	2−	2÷				3÷	4÷	10+
			16+					
4÷	2÷	6×		2−	16+		8−	7
		1−				72×		105×
3−			8×					

168×			3÷		13+	144×	
4÷	2÷	4÷		9			42×	2−
		30+					
2÷		42×	5−	4−	48×	8−	15×
15×	4−					2÷	7−
		7+			6		
4−	4−	270×		1120×		3÷	4÷
		19+					
17+		12+			8+	3÷	

5−	1−	28×		90×	6−		2−	8−
		7−				2−		
42×	13+		8−		60×		3÷	1−
		2÷		56×				
3+	6−	10×	4−		17+	12×	4−	2−
				54×				
360×			11+		3−	18+		
	7−			4		42×		
8	2÷		10+			18+		

2÷		8−		11+	10×	2−		3÷
45×	96×	3−				4−	2−	
			2÷	11+				17+
4÷		17+		1−		15+		
	7		2−				3÷	
945×		11+	14×	5−			200×	
2÷				2−		36×	8+	
			18+		11+			2÷
7−		30×				6×		

118 Moderate +/−/×/÷

192×			7+		6−		16+	
90×	13+	5−		6+		2−		
		24+			4−	6+		6×
	1−		1−			60×	24+	
8−	126×			2÷				
	4÷		5−		6−			13+
5−	2−	12+				2÷		
		36×		48×		1−		42×
80×				19+				

Moderate +/−/×/÷ 119

3−	2−		2÷		252×	288×	8+	
	12×	10+	16+					17+
8−				48×		75×		
		11+			30+			105×
7	8−					3÷		
2−	18+	8×		26+			12+	
		2−			3+			2÷
11+						1120×		
	13+		9+				5−	

120 Moderate +/−/×/÷

4÷		10×	8−		2−		4−	
6+			168×	3÷		19+		
	3÷				24×		7−	23+
2−	756×	8−		24×		18+		
		2÷		6−			5	
		3−		3÷			2÷	
1−	4−		17+		7−			
	17+			1−		2	8−	
54×			12×		6+		4÷	

Moderate +/−/×/÷ 121

21×	17+	96×			8−		11+	
			14+	60×		8+		3+
48×	36×	3+			21+			
			13+	4−	19+		18×	17+
3+	7	280×			17+			
	10+			7				
		8−	810×		3÷		1−	
4−	72×					2÷		
		12+			5−		4−	

54×		3−	8−	1−	14+			
4−				3÷	14+		2÷	
192×		63×		28+		3÷		
	105×						1134×	
40×		2−		2		8−		
16+	6+			7−		1−		
		1−			20+		175×	10+
8−		2−	48×	3÷				
1−						168×		

Moderate +/−/×/÷ 123

540×			16+		7−	84×	
3	160×			240×		2−	
4÷		168×					15×
	108×	210×	4−		216×	64×	
		8−					
63×		13+	6−				17+
	9+			18+		252×	
	2÷	13+					13+
24+							

120×			2÷		21+		336×	8−
3÷	48×	3−	17+					
			2160×		16+			
192×	4−			15+		6+		14+
	7−					6		
	1−				200×	14+		
14×	6+	8−		14+			22+	
					11+			3−
28×			48×		9			

3+	1−	1−		72×		36×	11+	11+
		5	17+	12+				
2−	3+			5−			2−	5−
	15+	10×			27+			
2÷			2−		3+		3÷	
		56×		2−			45×	3+
30+			5+		384×			
42×	4−					5−	1−	3−
		5−		2−				

48×		315×		8−		8×	84×	
21×			24+	48×	90×			6×
	11+	2÷				5−	3+	
7−				14+				13+
	120×					108×		
2−			4÷	1−	2−		7+	
23+		18×				16+	1890×	
			162×	1−	21+			

20×	3÷		7	3÷	14+	16+		
	2−	3+					4÷	8−
		378×			11+			
2÷		2−	90×			8−	64×	
3÷	8−		96×				1−	
		6−	17+			1−		
4÷				2÷			4−	
1−	12×				18+			1−
	4÷		13+			1−		

5−	4−		3+		30×		2÷	
	4−	24+		4÷	4−		3−	
18+					10×			2÷
		27+		6+		2÷		
3−			21+			3	8−	
17+				2−		3−		4÷
	2−	6×		4−	135×			
2÷		1−			17+		14×	
	8−		2÷		4−		2−	

4−	4−		12+	16×	20+				7−
	1−						1−		
2÷		8−		1−		14+			
17+	1440×	40×	15+	4	21×	8−	2÷	4−	
				3÷					
						16+	4−		
9+		3−		3−					
4−	8−		3÷	13+		1−		1−	
	54×				14+				

130 Moderate +/−/×/÷

72×	840×				8−		23+
		17+	35×	7−	2400×	1−	
12+	18+					24×	10+
		2−			16+		
		224×	28+	8−			
3−							2÷
	18+				1−		
8−	24×		144×			2−	5−
		48×			4		

26+		12×	14+		4−		5+	
			18+		40×	15+		8−
2÷		1−				12×		
3	23+	8−		14+	48×	14+		15×
		96×	7			2÷		
360×						36×		336×
		3÷		17+	21×	3−		
	48×	5−				15+		
			2−		2−		4÷	

132 Challenging +/−/×/÷

30×		22+					896×	
4−	72×	24×		240×			2÷	
			27+	4−	21+			
2÷							4÷	
3−			8×				2÷	
15+					3024×			
192×				1260×			10+	
8−	112×		112×		5+	2÷		19+
						8		

Challenging +/−/×/÷ 133

18+	3÷		1−		60×			6+
	36×		1−	72×		4÷		
	3−	7−			6−		189×	
168×			10+	45×	17+	13+		
	2−						18+	4
	3−	9+						
2			8−	48×	1−			23+
2−	1−					9+		
	3÷		2÷		126×			

1−	2÷		8−	72×	30×			2−
	20+	5−				18+		
			10+	3−	504×			2÷
3−		19+			30×		8×	
24×			1−					5
8+			2−	8−		10+		48×
336×		3÷					17+	
36×			4÷	882×				7+
	6+					2−		

18×		12+			72×		15+	
	8−		96×	35×	16+	4÷		
21+							252×	1
		2−			13+			
100×	504×			7−	24×			10+
		7−	1−		4−	4−	14+	
378×	2÷			6				144×
		1−	8−	2÷	3÷	12+		
	7							

136 Challenging +/−/×/÷

1−	30+				2÷		3÷	
	1890×			2	34+		54×	8+
6	8−		18+	30×	24+	588×	1440×	
2÷	6×							
	2÷							
22+		6+			21+	288×		1−
5−		6−						
	504×				6+		7−	

6	8−		5−	20×		6−	1344×	
360×			5−	14×				
9+		12+				1−		15+
	30+		15×		48×			
15+		6	2−		4÷		3÷	
		2−	12×		1−		8+	
			48×	1−	3÷	4−		
40×						1−	21×	
14+				18×				8

11+		42×		8−		2−	168×	
	7−	12+		5−				18+
5184×			270×	4÷	3−			
	24×				84×	4−		
		2÷	3−			1−		5
			15×	9+		54×		20+
	13+	56×			4÷			
35×				5−		240×		
		1−		2÷				

Challenging +/−/×/÷ 139

4−		189×			192×		13+	
384×	3÷	4÷		8−				105×
		25+	6×		9+			
	192×		5	16×			126×	36×
		7+	1	2−			
2−			24+				
	10+	4−		3÷		18+	
		72×	1−		600×	24×	
2−		1−					

3+		17+	17+			288×		63×
2−	9+				8+	6		
		2−		12×			180×	1−
336×	42×				21+			
	2−		8−			18+	4÷	
	72×			3÷				4−
5−	11+	4−			16+			
		24×		392×		15+		10+
8−			5					

Challenging +/−/×/÷ 141

3456×	2÷		540×			80×	22+	
		8+						4−
		24+					10+	
2−		112×			54×			11+
30+				4−		84×		
10+		30×	24×					
13+					1008×		2160×	20×
2÷		16+	36×	3	15+			

142 Challenging +/−/×/÷

6+	180×		252×			14+		8×
			126×				9	
10+			4÷	27+				
24+	13+		9+		17+	4−		10+
			10+					
5−		20×			2÷		42×	
17+	1−	1296×					2÷	126×
		8+		120×				
	1−		60×			2−		

2−		360×			3−		3÷	
12+			14+			19+		
25+		2−		17+			56×	9
		15+						
72×	72×		3−	3	2÷	10×		13+
	2−			144×		2−		
	6−		8−		28+	10+		
5−	28×							7+
	4−		108×			11+		

6+		252×			3÷		20+	
10+		560×		30+				
	9				1−			
224×	54×		32×			6×		8+
		84×	35×		6	28+		
			54×					
108×	40×		23+		27×	3−		20+
	96×			20×			19+	

Challenging +/−/×/÷ 145

3÷		252×	216×		24+		48×	
280×			1−					
		23+			2÷	9+		
12+	20×		7−					35+
	3÷		8−		7			
	3−	288×	12×		7−	11+		
315×	24×							
	8	28×	7−		20+			
6×						8−		

216×		6−	5−	7+		4−	20+	
				1−			15+	
19+	7−		8+		24×			1−
		216×	8−		12+	17+		
5			1−					11+
80×			2÷					
	3−		24×		10+		1−	
49×	1	24×	2−	40×		4÷		162×
			1−					

216×			8−	15+		120×		
3−	6×			17+		5−	120×	
	252×		14+		2÷		8+	
3÷								4÷
	2−	2160×	5−	2−	8−	6×	2÷	
2−								14×
			10+			2−		
16+			24+			36×		6
2÷		8				18+		

4÷		840×					6−	
2÷		24+	11+	3−	270×	28×	17+	
6+							6×	
18+				24+			160×	
					12+			
5−	2÷	30+				12+		8+
		2	21+	1−	3÷	640×		
24+		8+					21+	

4÷	2−		5−		24×			18+
	17+	24+			20+			
		16+				3÷		
8−	6×		3−		23+	840×	6−	16+
		288×						
756×		84×	24×					
				6×		3−		7−
1−		120×				5−		
	1−		3÷		5−		4÷	

150 Challenging +/−/×/÷

40×		1260×		14+			80×	
	3÷	5−		3−	8−	6−	24×	
144×								
	216×			144×	8+			56×
	6+				1120×			
11+		1296×					10+	
	224×	5				26+		162×
16+			112×	4−	16+			

ANSWERS

1

5− 6	4− 5	1	32× 2	4	8+ 3
1	2÷ 3	6	4	3÷ 2	5
5+ 4	1	8+ 3	5	6	3÷ 2
1− 3	2	3− 4	1	15× 5	6
3− 5	2− 4	2	6 6	3	5+ 1
2	11+ 6	5	3÷ 3	1	4

2

3÷ 1	3	24× 6	4	7+ 5	2
2− 3	5− 6	6+ 5	1	8× 2	24× 4
5	1	8+ 3	2 2	4	6
240× 2	4	1	11+ 5	6	45× 3
4	5	3÷ 2	6	3	1
6	8× 2	4	3÷ 3	1	5

3

5− 1	6	**3** 3	**40×** 4	5	2
10+ 4	**5+** 1	**11+** 5	6	**5+** 2	**12+** 3
6	4	**2÷** 2	1	3	5
30× 2	**3÷** 3	1	**11+** 5	6	4
3	5	**2÷** 4	2	**5−** 1	6
3− 5	2	**2÷** 6	3	**5+** 4	1

4

90× 3	**3+** 1	2	**10+** 6	4	**15+** 5
6	**3÷** 3	1	**7+** 2	5	4
1	5	**2÷** 3	**1−** 4	**3+** 2	6
160× 5	4	6	3	1	**3+** 2
2	**2−** 6	4	**8+** 5	3	1
4	**7+** 2	5	**5−** 1	6	**3** 3

5

6+ 5	1	3− 6	3	48× 4	2
1− 3	4	60× 5	3+ 1	2	6
2÷ 4	6	2	11+ 5	9× 1	3
2	60× 5	4	6	3	1 1
3+ 1	2	3	480× 4	6	5
3− 6	3	2÷ 1	2	5 5	4

6

60× 5	18× 1	6	3	4 4	3÷ 2
3	2÷ 4	2	4− 5	3+ 1	6
4	11+ 6	5	1	2	15× 3
5− 6	2÷ 2	1	2÷ 4	2÷ 3	5
1	2− 5	3	2	6	20× 4
1− 2	3	24× 4	6	5	1

4− 5	**2÷** 6	**5−** 1	**2÷** 4	**1−** 3	2
1	3	6	2	**20×** 4	5
7+ 4	**6×** 2	3	1	**11+** 5	**5−** 6
3	**11+** 4	2	5	6	1
3÷ 6	**4−** 1	**1−** 5	**3−** 3	**2÷** 2	4
2	5	4	6	**3÷** 1	3

5+ 1	4	**11+** 6	5	**6×** 2	3
2− 5	**5−** 1	**11+** 4	3	**30×** 6	**2÷** 2
3	6	**2** 2	4	5	1
24× 6	**2−** 3	5	**3+** 2	1	**20×** 4
4	**20×** 2	**3÷** 1	**5−** 6	**13+** 3	5
2	5	3	1	4	6

9

3+ 2	**12×** 4	3	**6+** 5	1	**3−** 6
1	**17+** 2	6	4	5	3
2÷ 6	3	**3−** 2	**3÷** 1	**1−** 4	5
1− 4	**11+** 6	5	3	**3÷** 2	**3−** 1
3	5	**8×** 1	2	6	4
6+ 5	1	4	**6** 6	**5+** 3	2

10

1− 4	3	**3÷** 6	2	**2−** 5	**5+** 1
2÷ 6	**10×** 2	5	1	3	4
3	**5−** 6	**7+** 2	4	1	**11+** 5
3+ 2	1	**12+** 3	5	4	6
1	**9+** 5	4	**3** 3	**3÷** 6	**5+** 2
1− 5	4	**5−** 1	6	2	3

11

³ 3	¹¹⁺ 5	6	^{48×} 4	^{2÷} 1	2
^{5−} 6	1	4	3	⁸⁺ 2	5
^{20×} 5	4	⁵⁺ 3	^{3÷} 2	6	1
^{1−} 4	3	2	^{15×} 1	5	^{2−} 6
^{4×} 1	2	¹¹⁺ 5	6	3	4
2	⁷⁺ 6	1	⁵ 5	^{1−} 4	3

12

^{2÷} 4	^{18×} 1	6	3	⁷⁺ 2	5
2	¹¹⁺ 3	¹⁰⁺ 4	6	⁶⁺ 5	1
^{5−} 6	2	1	5	^{2÷} 3	^{1−} 4
1	¹⁵⁺ 4	5	² 2	6	3
^{75×} 5	6	^{2−} 3	1	^{2÷} 4	2
3	5	^{2÷} 2	4	^{5−} 1	6

13

2÷ **1**	24× **4**	**6**	3− **5**	**2**	90× **3**
2	**1**	1− **5**	2÷ **4**	3÷ **3**	**6**
2÷ **6**	**3**	**4**	**2**	**1**	**5**
12+ **4**	2÷ **6**	**3**	4− **1**	**5**	8× **2**
3	3− **5**	**2**	10+ **6**	**4**	**1**
5	3+ **2**	**1**	3− **3**	**6**	**4**

14

4 **4**	1− **6**	**5**	6× **3**	**1**	**2**
3+ **1**	**2**	2÷ **6**	3− **5**	60× **4**	**3**
15+ **6**	**4**	**3**	**2**	**5**	5− **1**
5	2÷ **1**	**2**	13+ **4**	**3**	**6**
30× **2**	3 **3**	5+ **4**	5− **1**	**6**	40× **5**
3	**5**	**1**	**6**	**2**	**4**

15

6 ₆	**1** _{3÷}	**3**	**2** _{3−}	**5**	**4** _{1−}
1 ₃₊	**2**	**5** _{40×}	**6** _{2−}	**4**	**3**
5 _{2−}	**3**	**2**	**4**	**1** _{5−}	**6**
2 _{2−}	**4**	**6** _{120×}	**5**	**3** _{3÷}	**1**
3 _{72×}	**6**	**4**	**1** ₃₊	**2**	**5** _{10×}
4	**5** _{4−}	**1**	**3** _{2÷}	**6**	**2**

16

6 _{3÷}	**4** _{20×}	**3** _{1−}	**2**	**5** ₁₀₊	**1**
2	**5**	**6** _{30×}	**4** ₅₊	**1**	**3**
4 ₁₀₊	**6**	**5**	**1**	**3** _{1−}	**2** _{3÷}
5 _{3−}	**2**	**1** _{2÷}	**3** _{15×}	**4**	**6**
3 ₃	**1** _{3×}	**2**	**5**	**6** _{3÷}	**4** _{1−}
1	**3**	**4** _{2−}	**6**	**2**	**5**

17

2÷ 1	15+ 5	12× 4	60× 2	2÷ 3	6
2	4	3	5	6	1 1
360× 5	6	3− 1	4	5+ 2	3
3	6× 1	3÷ 2	6	1− 5	4
4	2	1− 6	15× 3	1	5
6	3	5	1	2÷ 4	2

18

40× 2	4	5	10+ 3	6	1
4− 1	5	13+ 3	12× 6	2÷ 4	2
11+ 5	6	4	2	1	7+ 3
6	3+ 2	1	2− 5	3	4
12× 3	5− 1	6	2− 4	2	11+ 5
4	5+ 3	2	4− 1	5	6

19

5	4−		3÷		120×
5	**6**	**2**	**1**	**3**	**4**
15+ 4	**3**	**5+** 1	**3÷** 2	**6**	**5**
3	**5**	**4**	**6**	**2÷** 2	**1**
3÷ 6	**2**	**11+** 5	**1−** 4	**3÷** 1	**3**
8× 1	**4**	**6**	**3**	**60×** 5	**2**
2	**3÷** 1	**3**	**1−** 5	**4**	**6**

20

6+		2÷		2÷	
5	**1**	**4**	**2**	**3**	**6**
5− 1	**24×** 2	**360×** 5	**6**	**4**	**3**
6	**4**	**3**	**5+** 1	**1−** 5	**2÷** 2
1− 3	**3−** 5	**2**	**4**	**6**	**1**
2	**3−** 3	**6**	**20×** 5	**1**	**4**
24× 4	**6**	**3÷** 1	**3**	**3−** 2	**5**

21

50× 5	2÷ 4	2	5− 1	6	8+ 3
2	5	3− 3	6	4	1
2− 4	6	1 1	20× 5	1− 3	2
5− 1	1− 3	60× 5	4	2÷ 2	11+ 6
6	2	4	3	1	5
3÷ 3	1	3÷ 6	2	1− 5	4

22

24× 4	1− 5	4− 1	2÷ 6	3	1− 2
6	4	5	3+ 2	1	3
1− 3	2	20× 4	5	48× 6	1
2− 5	3	5− 6	1	2	4
2÷ 2	5− 1	1− 3	20× 4	5	11+ 6
1	6	2	7+ 3	4	5

360× 5	3	2÷ 4	5− 6	1	1− 2
6	4	2	15× 5	3	1
9+ 4	5	1− 6	3÷ 1	1− 2	3
3+ 2	1	5	3	2− 4	6
3 3	9+ 2	3÷ 1	10+ 4	6	20× 5
1	6	3	3− 2	5	4

5− 6	60× 3	2÷ 2	4	1 1	7+ 5
1	5	4	2÷ 6	3	2
1− 4	1− 6	5	2÷ 1	2	72× 3
5	2÷ 2	1	7+ 3	4	6
3 3	18× 1	6	12+ 2	5	4
2÷ 2	4	3	5	7+ 6	1

25

2÷ **6**	**3**	1− **1**	**2**	1− **4**	**5**
12× **1**	**6**	**2**	72× **4**	15× **5**	**3**
15× **5**	**1**	**3**	**6**	16× **2**	**4**
15+ **4**	**5**	**6**	**3**	**1**	**2**
7+ **2**	1− **4**	**5**	**1**	18× **3**	6 **6**
3	**2**	20× **4**	**5**	**6**	**1**

26

6× **3**	1− **6**	6+ **5**	**1**	2− **4**	**2**
2	**5**	10+ **1**	**6**	**3**	3− **4**
15+ **5**	**4**	**6**	5+ **3**	**2**	**1**
11+ **6**	**3**	**2**	5+ **4**	**1**	2− **5**
3− **1**	2÷ **2**	15+ **4**	**5**	**6**	**3**
4	**1**	1− **3**	**2**	11+ **5**	**6**

3–		36×		12×	9+
5	**2**	**6**	**3**	**1**	**4**
24×					
1	**6**	**2**	**4**	**3**	**5**
2÷		3+		2–	
6	**4**	**1**	**2**	**5**	**3**
	10+	3–		4–	
3	**5**	**4**	**1**	**2**	**6**
		90×	120×		2÷
4	**1**	**3**	**5**	**6**	**2**
1–					
2	**3**	**5**	**6**	**4**	**1**

4–		15×		1–	
6	**2**	**5**	**1**	**4**	**3**
1–	3÷				4–
4	**6**	**2**	**3**	**1**	**5**
	12+	1–		12+	
5	**4**	**3**	**2**	**6**	**1**
		5–			
3	**5**	**1**	**6**	**2**	**4**
1	13+		14+		36×
1	**3**	**6**	**4**	**5**	**2**
3+					
2	**1**	**4**	**5**	**3**	**6**

29

36× 2	**3÷** 1	3	**1−** 5	6	**13+** 4
3	6	**4−** 1	**2÷** 2	4	5
96× 6	4	5	1	**8+** 3	2
4	**3−** 5	2	**5−** 6	1	3
3+ 1	2	**1−** 4	3	**1−** 5	6
8+ 5	3	**2−** 6	4	**1−** 2	1

30

4 4	**11+** 6	5	**3÷** 3	1	**60×** 2
5− 1	**11+** 5	2	4	**3** 3	6
6	**1−** 3	4	**2÷** 1	2	5
60× 3	**10+** 4	6	**3−** 2	5	**12×** 1
5	2	**11+** 1	6	4	3
2	**3÷** 1	3	**11+** 5	6	4

31

24× 4	**6×** 1	2	3	**1−** 5	6
1	**3÷** 6	**5** 5	**30×** 2	3	**12×** 4
6	2	**3−** 1	5	**24×** 4	3
30× 2	**10+** 3	4	**12×** 1	6	**4−** 5
5	4	3	6	2	1
3	**15+** 5	6	4	**2÷** 1	2

32

3÷ 2	**1−** 3	4	**5−** 6	1	**20×** 5
6	**4−** 1	5	**1−** 3	2	4
4− 5	**2÷** 2	1	**7+** 4	3	**3÷** 6
1	**9+** 4	**2÷** 3	**3−** 5	**2−** 6	2
7+ 3	5	6	2	4	**3÷** 1
4	**4−** 6	2	**4−** 1	5	3

33

15× **3**	**5**	10+ **6**	32× **4**	1− **2**	**1**
120× **5**	**1**	**3**	**2**	**4**	10+ **6**
6	**4**	3− **2**	**5**	**1**	**3**
2÷ **4**	2÷ **6**	3÷ **1**	**3**	1− **5**	3− **2**
2	**3**	3− **4**	**1**	**6**	**5**
2÷ **1**	**2**	1− **5**	**6**	1− **3**	**4**

34

1− **2**	15× **1**	**3**	**5**	12+ **4**	24× **6**
1	60× **2**	**5**	**6**	**3**	**4**
2− **6**	**4**	3÷ **2**	6+ **3**	**5**	**1**
1− **4**	**5**	**6**	**2**	9+ **1**	**3**
2− **3**	2− **6**	**4**	**1**	10+ **2**	**5**
5	3 **3**	3− **1**	**4**	**6**	**2**

35

40× 4	5	10+ 6	2÷ 2	9+ 1	3
2	13+ 4	3	1	6 6	5
1− 6	3	1	4 4	1− 5	2÷ 2
5	6	6× 2	3	4	1
3÷ 3	1	11+ 5	6	2− 2	4
2÷ 1	2	9+ 4	5	2÷ 3	6

36

2− 5	3	10+ 6	1	360× 2	1− 4
12× 4	2	1	6	5	3
3	1− 4	5	9+ 2	6	5− 1
1	8+ 5	2	3	4	6
6 6	1	48× 4	9+ 5	3	3− 2
3÷ 2	6	3	4	1	5

37

60× 4	**3÷** 6	2	**3÷** 1	3	**8+** 5
3	5	**5−** 6	**15+** 4	1	2
9+ 5	2	1	6	**8+** 4	3
2	**18×** 3	**4** 4	5	**48×** 6	1
6	1	**2−** 5	**1−** 3	2	4
5+ 1	4	3	2	**30×** 5	6

38

15× 3	5	**3−** 1	4	**15+** 6	**3÷** 2
2− 4	2	3	1	5	6
2÷ 2	**2−** 6	4	**3−** 3	**6+** 1	5
1	**8+** 3	5	6	**2÷** 2	4
5− 6	1	**120×** 2	5	4	**2−** 3
1− 5	4	**3÷** 6	2	3	1

39

12× 1	3	8+ 5	3÷ 2	10+ 6	4
4	2	1	6	9+ 5	3
1− 6	2− 4	5+ 2	3	1	3− 5
5	6	2− 3	1	12× 4	2
1− 2	1− 5	6	1− 4	3	1
3	5+ 1	4	5	3÷ 2	6

40

24× 2	3	1− 5	6	6+ 1	4
4	1− 2	3	1− 5	6	1
8+ 6	1	1− 4	3	50× 5	2
1	18+ 6	2÷ 2	4	108× 3	5
5	4	12+ 6	7+ 1	2	3
3	5	1	2	4	6

41

4− 5	24× 4	6	1− 2	3	2÷ 1
1	2− 3	5	2− 6	4	2
2÷ 4	2	2− 3	5	5− 1	6
1− 6	5	3− 4	1	1− 2	3
1− 3	5− 1	2÷ 2	4	1− 6	9+ 5
2	6	3÷ 1	3	5	4

42

30× 1	5	1− 3	20× 4	3÷ 6	2
6	1	4	5	1− 2	3
15+ 4	6	5	1− 2	3	6+ 1
24× 3	4	2	6× 6	1	5
20× 5	2	5− 1	3÷ 3	2− 4	6
2	3 3	6	1	20× 5	4

43

4− **1**	**5**	1− **3**	**2**	2− **4**	**6**
5+ **2**	9+ **6**	**1**	1− **3**	20× **5**	**4**
3	**2**	30× **6**	**4**	6+ **1**	5 **5**
1− **4**	7+ **1**	**5**	6× **6**	**3**	**2**
5	**4**	**2**	**1**	2÷ **6**	**3**
3− **6**	**3**	9+ **4**	**5**	2÷ **2**	**1**

44

36× **6**	5 **5**	6+ **2**	**3**	**1**	40× **4**
3	**2**	2÷ **6**	3− **1**	2− **4**	**5**
6+ **5**	**1**	**3**	**4**	**6**	**2**
3÷ **2**	**6**	1− **4**	1− **5**	1− **3**	15+ **1**
48× **1**	**4**	**5**	**6**	**2**	**3**
4	**3**	2÷ **1**	**2**	**5**	**6**

45

3÷ **6**	**2**	20× **5**	**4**	3÷ **1**	**3**
14+ **3**	**6**	5− **1**	7+ **5**	9+ **2**	**4**
9+ **4**	**5**	**6**	**2**	**3**	2÷ **1**
5	72× **3**	**4**	**1**	**6**	**2**
2÷ **2**	**1**	2÷ **3**	**6**	1− **4**	**5**
3− **1**	**4**	1− **2**	**3**	1− **5**	**6**

46

72× **4**	5− **1**	**6**	8+ **2**	3 **3**	12+ **5**
3	5 **5**	**2**	**4**	**6**	**1**
6	13+ **3**	8+ **5**	7+ **1**	2÷ **2**	**4**
14+ **5**	**4**	**3**	**6**	2÷ **1**	**2**
2	**6**	9+ **1**	**5**	1− **4**	**3**
1	**2**	**4**	**3**	1− **5**	**6**

47

5 5	**3−** 1	4	**12×** 2	6	**12+** 3
3− 3	**3÷** 6	**8+** 2	5	1	4
6	2	**2−** 3	1	**2÷** 4	5
2÷ 4	**12×** 3	5	**18×** 6	2	**1** 1
2	4	1	3	**60×** 5	**3÷** 6
30× 1	5	6	4	3	2

48

60× 5	4	3	**2÷** 1	2	**5−** 6
11+ 4	2	**2÷** 6	3	**6+** 5	1
3÷ 6	5	**2−** 2	4	1	**12×** 3
2	**18×** 6	**4−** 1	5	**7+** 3	4
1	3	**1−** 5	6	4	**3−** 2
3 3	**5+** 1	4	**4−** 2	6	5

49

2÷ 6	2÷ 1	2	1− 3	4	7+ 5
3	6+ 5	1	24× 4	6	2
3− 5	2	2− 6	6+ 1	1− 3	4
3÷ 2	6	4	5	2− 1	3
3− 1	4	8+ 3	3÷ 2	30× 5	6
7+ 4	3	5	6	1− 2	1

50

16+ 5	72× 1	2	3	6	7+ 4
4	2÷ 3	6	30× 5	2	1
3	4	17+ 5	6	1	2
5− 1	6	4	10× 2	5	14+ 3
24× 2	5	3	1	48× 4	6
6	2	1	4	3	5

51

13+		40×		9+		
7	**6**	**2**	**4**	**5**	**1**	**3**
2÷			252×		3	35×
2	**4**	**5**	**7**	**6**	**3**	**1**
2÷	11+			6−		
3	**2**	**4**	**6**	**1**	**7**	**5**
		3÷		2−		
6	**5**	**3**	**1**	**2**	**4**	**7**
60×		14×			144×	
5	**3**	**1**	**2**	**7**	**6**	**4**
	6−		30×			
4	**1**	**7**	**5**	**3**	**2**	**6**
6−		72×			10×	
1	**7**	**6**	**3**	**4**	**5**	**2**

52

105×		2÷		6−		5−
3	**5**	**2**	**4**	**7**	**1**	**6**
	14+	11+			300×	
7	**4**	**3**	**6**	**2**	**5**	**1**
24×			3÷			11+
4	**2**	**5**	**3**	**1**	**6**	**7**
		6−				
6	**3**	**7**	**1**	**5**	**2**	**4**
5−		12+			14×	
1	**6**	**4**	**5**	**3**	**7**	**2**
7+	6−		2	72×		15×
5	**7**	**1**	**2**	**6**	**4**	**3**
	1	168×				
2	**1**	**6**	**7**	**4**	**3**	**5**

53

2− 4	2	6− 1	7	90× 6	5	3
15× 1	5	3	168× 2	13+ 7	6	16+ 4
3÷ 2	3÷ 1	30× 6	4	3	7	5
6	3	5	6× 1	32× 4	2	7
5 5	1176× 7	2	3	1	4	5− 6
7	6	4	210× 5	30× 2	3	1
1− 3	4	7	6	5	1− 1	2

54

6− 1	7	12× 3	4	3− 5	2	2− 6
12× 3	10× 5	1	14× 7	2	2÷ 6	4
4	2	12+ 5	1	6	3	14+ 7
28× 7	4	3÷ 6	2	3× 3	1	5
30× 5	3 3	13+ 7	6	1	28× 4	2
6	3+ 1	2	1− 5	4	7	3÷ 3
3÷ 2	6	4 4	15+ 3	7	5	1

55

1− 4	13+ 6	7	1− 5	6× 1	3	2
3	2÷ 2	5+ 1	6	1− 7	3− 5	7+ 4
5 5	1	4	6− 7	6	2	3
3÷ 6	14× 7	2	1	1− 3	4	5 5
2	8+ 5	30× 6	3 3	2÷ 4	5− 1	8+ 7
6− 7	3	5	2÷ 4	2	6	1
1	7+ 4	3	2	210× 5	7	6

56

20× 2	5	144× 6	4	6− 7	3÷ 1	3
10+ 5	2	15× 3	6	1	2− 4	7 7
1	4	5	4− 7	3	6	10× 2
13+ 6	7	1− 4	5	5+ 2	3	1
14+ 4	1 1	6− 7	2÷ 3	6	60× 2	5
7	2÷ 3	1	4× 2	1− 4	5	6
3	6	2	1	5	28× 7	4

7+	13+	3÷		3÷	35×	
4	6	3	1	2	7	5
3	7	120× 4	5	6	6× 2	1
2÷ 2	1	6	13+ 7	15× 5	3	24× 4
3− 7	4	6− 1	6	3	120× 5	2
7+ 5	2	7	9+ 4	1	6	3
5− 1	2− 5	2	3	3− 7	4	6 6
6	3	3− 5	2	4	6− 1	7

90×			2÷		3−	
3	5	6	1	2	7	4
1− 4	2÷ 2	1	18+ 6	7	5	14+ 3
5	21× 3	4 4	6− 7	1	2÷ 2	6
7	1	11+ 2	3	6	4	5
14× 2	7	60× 3	4	5	5− 6	1
120× 6	4	5	3− 2	3 3	6− 1	7
1 1	13+ 6	7	5	24× 4	3	2

59

2÷ 2	4	**24×** 1	**11+** 5	**2÷** 6	3	**13+** 7
4− 7	3	4	2	**6−** 1	**5** 5	6
120× 5	**14+** 2	6	4	7	**3+** 1	**60×** 3
6	5	7	**3÷** 1	3	2	4
4	**6×** 1	3	**13+** 7	**60×** 2	6	5
3 3	**42×** 7	2	6	5	**112×** 4	**2÷** 1
1	6	**2−** 5	3	4	7	2

60

18+ 6	**84×** 3	4	7	**20×** 5	**1−** 2	1
5	**3+** 1	**10×** 2	**5−** 6	4	**14+** 7	**2÷** 3
7	2	5	1	3	4	6
24× 4	6	**6−** 7	**2÷** 2	1	**8+** 3	5
6× 3	**1−** 5	1	**1−** 4	**18+** 7	6	**5−** 2
1	4	**14+** 6	3	**3÷** 2	5	7
2	**7** 7	3	5	6	**5+** 1	4

61

525× 7	3	5	**4−** 6	**2÷** 4	2	**11+** 1
3+ 1	5	**17+** 3	2	**13+** 7	6	4
2	**12+** 1	7	4	3	**20×** 5	6
15× 5	7	4	**3−** 3	6	1	**9+** 2
3	**2** 2	**12+** 6	5	1	4	7
288× 4	6	2	**6−** 1	**105×** 5	7	3
6	**5+** 4	1	7	**10+** 2	3	5

62

1− 3	**1−** 4	5	**5−** 7	2	**1−** 6	**3+** 1
4	**4−** 6	**5−** 1	**105×** 3	7	5	2
6− 1	2	6	5	**13+** 3	**4** 4	**210×** 7
7	**3+** 1	2	**4** 4	6	**5+** 3	5
17+ 5	7	**1−** 3	**8+** 1	4	2	6
3÷ 2	5	4	6	1	**8+** 7	**7+** 3
6	**10+** 3	7	**7+** 2	5	1	4

63

21× 7	2 2	24× 6	1	4	10+ 5	3
3	6− 7	1	15+ 5	6	4	2
3÷ 2	10+ 5	4	6− 7	1	6× 3	1− 6
6	1	14+ 7	4	3	2	5
20× 4	3÷ 6	2	5+ 3	4− 5	1	8+ 7
5	12+ 4	3	2	13+ 7	6	1
3÷ 1	3	5	3÷ 6	2	11+ 7	4

64

13+ 7	6	105× 3	56× 2	4	1	19+ 5
40× 2	1	5	7	60× 3	4	6
4	105× 3	7	1	5	6	2
5	7	4 4	144× 6	3+ 1	2	11+ 3
2÷ 3	5	3+ 2	4	6	7	1
6	13+ 2	1	150× 5	21× 7	3	3− 4
1	4	6	3	2	5	7

12× 4	5 5	3÷ 3	1	13+ 6	7	13+ 2
1	3	3÷ 6	10+ 5	2	4	7
1− 5	4	2	7 7	3	5− 1	6
3÷ 6	6− 1	84× 7	3	4	1− 2	20× 5
2	7	240× 5	6	6− 1	3	4
21× 3	3÷ 6	4	2	7	1− 5	3÷ 1
7	2	20× 1	4	5	6	3

2÷ 4	300× 2	5	6− 7	1	2÷ 6	3
2	4 4	6	5	15+ 7	120× 3	4− 1
294× 7	3÷ 1	3	6	2	4	5
6	7	2 2	8+ 3	5	1	3− 4
15× 1	1− 3	4	2 2	10+ 6	5	7
3	20+ 5	7	1	4	2	84× 6
5	6	1	1− 4	3	7	2

67

³÷ 6	2	⁷²ˣ 3	³⁵ˣ 7	²⁸ˣ 4	⁴⁻ 5	1
⁸⁺ 2	4	6	5	7	1	¹³⁺ 3
5	1	¹⁵⁺ 4	6	2	3	7
¹³⁺ 7	6	² 2	3	²⁰ˣ 1	4	5
²⁰ˣ 1	¹²⁺ 3	5	4	¹³⁺ 6	7	¹⁰⁺ 2
4	5	²¹ˣ 7	1	3	2	6
⁴⁻ 3	7	⁸⁺ 1	2	5	¹⁰⁺ 6	4

68

³⁰ˣ 2	5	⁴²ˣ 6	¹⁰⁺ 4	²÷ 3	¹⁴ˣ 1	7
⁶⁻ 1	3	7	5	6	2	¹⁻ 4
7	⁷⁺ 2	5	1	¹⁰⁺ 4	6	3
¹²ˣ 6	1	2	³⁶ˣ 3	¹⁶⁺ 7	4	5
⁴⁻ 3	7	¹¹⁺ 4	2	¹⁰⁺ 1	¹¹⁺ 5	6
¹⁵⁺ 5	4	3	6	2	7	⁶⁺ 1
4	6	⁶⁻ 1	7	⁵ 5	3	2

6− 1	7	13+ 6	1− 3	2÷ 4	2	20× 5
3− 6	5+ 1	7	2	75× 3	5	4
3	4	7+ 1	13+ 7	5	2÷ 6	4− 2
2− 7	5	4	1	2 2	3	6
2÷ 4	3− 6	2	5	28× 7	2− 1	3
2	3	2− 5	2− 6	1	4	6− 7
3− 5	2	3	4	13+ 6	7	1

2÷ 4	72× 3	1− 7	6	70× 2	5	10× 1
2	6	4	1− 3	7	6− 1	5
17+ 6	4− 1	5	4	13+ 3	7	2
1	5	9+ 2	7	4	2÷ 6	3
5	6− 7	1	3+ 2	6	1− 3	168× 4
4− 3	2− 4	6 6	1	20× 5	2	7
7	2	2− 3	5	1	4	6

71

1− **3**	40× **2**	13+ **6**	**7**	16+ **1**	**5**	3− **4**
2	**4**	**5**	30× **6**	**7**	**3**	**1**
6− **1**	1− **3**	**4**	**5**	3÷ **2**	**6**	2− **7**
7	4− **6**	**2**	2− **3**	5+ **4**	**1**	**5**
84× **4**	**7**	**3**	**1**	2− **5**	3÷ **2**	**6**
11+ **6**	**5**	**1**	2÷ **4**	**3**	5− **7**	**2**
5 **5**	6− **1**	**7**	**2**	13+ **6**	**4**	**3**

72

6− **1**	2÷ **4**	**2**	1− **7**	**6**	2− **5**	**3**
7	40× **5**	**4**	**2**	2÷ **3**	**6**	8+ **1**
13+ **2**	1 **1**	14+ **6**	12× **4**	2− **5**	**3**	**7**
6	2÷ **3**	**7**	**1**	4 **4**	3− **2**	**5**
5	**6**	**1**	**3**	3− **7**	**4**	2÷ **2**
12× **3**	18+ **7**	**5**	**6**	2÷ **2**	**1**	**4**
4	5+ **2**	**3**	4− **5**	**1**	1− **7**	**6**

73

3+ 1	1- 4	126× 6	3	7	60× 2	1- 5
2	3	6- 7	1	6	5	4
2- 7	3+ 2	12+ 5	4	3	2- 6	7+ 1
5	1	3 3	5- 7	2	4	6
13+ 3	3- 7	4	30× 6	4- 5	1	12+ 2
4	3÷ 6	2	5	6- 1	7	3
6	4- 5	1	2 2	1- 4	3	7

74

6- 1	13+ 6	2	4- 7	2- 4	10+ 5	6× 3
7	6+ 1	5	3	6	4	2
3	2	2- 6	4	105× 5	1	17+ 7
16+ 6	5	6- 7	2÷ 1	3	2 2	4
5	12× 4	1	2	7	16+ 3	6
672× 2	3	4	1- 6	1- 1	7	6+ 5
4	7	3	5	2	6	1

75

2− 4	35× 5	3+ 1	2	3 3	13+ 7	2− 6
2	7	12+ 5	3	3+ 1	6	4
24× 6	1	4	7 7	2	30× 3	5
6− 7	4	2÷ 6	3− 1	35× 5	2	1− 3
1	14+ 6	3	4	7	35× 5	2
5	3	12+ 2	6	4	1	7
1− 3	2	210× 7	5	6	3− 4	1

76

24× 4	11+ 5	1	1− 6	7	1− 2	3
1	6	5	2÷ 2	1− 3	4	840× 7
36× 2	252× 3	7 7	1	4	6	5
6	7	3	5 5	2÷ 2	3− 1	4
3	4	168× 6	7	1	60× 5	2
6− 7	1	80× 2	4	2− 5	3	6
5	2	4	2÷ 3	6	6− 7	1

2− 7	2− 6	4	90× 3	5	8× 1	2
5	1− 7	6	1	2	3	4
13+ 4	2	7	14+ 5	2÷ 3	6	10+ 1
10+ 6	4	5 5	2	6− 1	7	3
6+ 2	3	1	7	1− 4	5	6
3÷ 3	2÷ 1	2	1008× 6	7	4	14+ 5
1	12+ 5	3	4	6	2	7

5− 7	20× 5	4	1	3÷ 2	6	2÷ 3
2	16+ 7	5	3− 4	1	42× 3	6
24× 6	4	22+ 1	5	3 3	2	7
4	2÷ 6	3	7	18+ 5	1− 1	2
1	6× 3	7	2	6	13+ 5	4
2− 3	1	2	3− 6	7	4	4− 5
5	3÷ 2	6	3	3− 4	7	1

79

3÷ **3**	140× **7**	**5**	2÷ **2**	**1**	2÷ **4**	2÷ **6**
1	**4**	25+ **7**	**5**	**6**	**2**	**3**
11+ **5**	6× **2**	2− **6**	**4**	**7**	10+ **3**	5+ **1**
6	**1**	**3**	6− **7**	**2**	**5**	**4**
12+ **2**	**6**	**4**	**1**	15+ **3**	**7**	**5**
28× **7**	4− **5**	**1**	2÷ **3**	2− **4**	**6**	5− **2**
4	1− **3**	**2**	**6**	4− **5**	**1**	**7**

80

4− **3**	3÷ **6**	12+ **4**	5− **7**	**2**	30× **5**	3− **1**
7	**2**	**5**	**3**	**1**	**6**	**4**
30× **6**	**5**	1− **3**	**2**	17+ **4**	6− **1**	**7**
1− **5**	**4**	6− **7**	**1**	**6**	**2**	3 **3**
6× **2**	**3**	3− **1**	**4**	**5**	1− **7**	**6**
3− **4**	6− **1**	3÷ **6**	5 **5**	84× **7**	**3**	7+ **2**
1	**7**	**2**	2÷ **6**	**3**	**4**	**5**

81

⁴⁻5	³÷6	2	²⁴ˣ8	3	³⁻4	7	⁶⁻1
1	²÷3	6	¹⁵⁺4	³⁵ˣ5	⁴÷8	2	7
⁵⁶ˣ2	²⁴ˣ8	3	5	7	²⁴ˣ1	6	4
4	7	¹⁻5	6	1	²÷3	⁴÷8	2
³⁵ˣ7	5	4	¹⁻3	³÷2	6	⁷⁻1	8
²÷3	¹1	²³⁺8	2	6	¹⁴ˣ7	⁶⁰ˣ4	5
6	⁶⁴ˣ4	7	⁷⁻1	8	2	¹⁴⁺5	3
8	2	1	7	¹⁻4	5	3	6

82

⁴⁻1	5	²÷4	²⁻3	⁶ˣ2	¹¹⁺7	²¹⁺6	⁸8
²⁻5	7	2	1	3	4	8	²⁴ˣ6
²⁻6	¹⁸⁺3	8	2	5	¹⁻1	7	4
4	⁷⁻8	1	¹⁻7	6	2	¹⁰ˣ5	³÷3
⁴⁻7	²÷6	3	⁴⁻8	4	⁴⁰ˣ5	2	1
3	¹⁴⁺2	5	6	1	8	⁸⁺4	⁷⁰ˣ7
²÷2	1	¹⁻7	¹⁻4	¹⁵⁺8	²÷6	3	5
⁴⁻8	4	6	5	7	3	1	2

83

26+ 7	1− 6	5	56× 8	8× 1	4	6× 2	3
6	13+ 8	3	7	2	16+ 5	6+ 1	7+ 4
8	10+ 3	2	16+ 6	4	7	5	1
5	7	6	4	2÷ 3	3÷ 1	21+ 8	2
24× 2	20× 5	6− 7	1	6	3	4	280× 8
1	4	13+ 8	2	21+ 7	6	3	5
4	2	1	15× 3	15+ 5	8	6	7
3	4÷ 1	4	5	8	2	13+ 7	6

84

2− 6	42× 1	7	1− 4	5	4− 3	4÷ 8	2
4	6	6+ 1	3	2	7	3− 5	8
7 7	15+ 5	6	2	7− 8	1	10+ 4	7+ 3
5− 3	8	2	1− 7	6	5	1	4
2− 5	3	18+ 8	7+ 6	1	32× 4	3÷ 2	12+ 7
16× 8	7	3	1 1	4	2	6	5
2	32× 4	280× 5	8	7	2− 6	3÷ 3	1
1	2	4	8+ 5	3	8	13+ 7	6

4÷ 4	26+ 6	105× 3	280× 5	7	8	3- 2	6× 1
1	8	7	3÷ 3	4- 4	13+ 2	5	6
1- 3	7	5	1	8	6	96× 4	2 2
2	5	2- 6	1- 7	1	4	3	8
42× 6	10+ 2	4	8	105× 5	3	280× 1	7
7	4	11+ 2	2- 6	1- 3	1	8	5
13+ 5	1	8	4	2	7	13+ 6	1- 3
8	3	1	13+ 2	6	5	7	4

3÷ 1	3	35× 7	2÷ 4	2	19+ 8	1- 5	6
2÷ 3	6	1	5	4	7	6- 2	8
17+ 8	7	10+ 4	6	2÷ 1	2	15× 3	5
2	19+ 8	3	2- 7	5	120× 4	6	1
112× 7	4	8	2÷ 3	6	5	10+ 1	2
4	16+ 5	6	16× 2	18+ 3	7- 1	8	7
13+ 6	2	5	1	8	2÷ 3	84× 7	4
5	2÷ 1	2	8	7	6	4 4	3

87

24× 6	4	1− 1	10× 2	4− 7	7+ 3	3− 5	8
35× 7	6− 1	2	5	3	4	4− 8	3÷ 6
5	7	2÷ 3	6	16× 8	1	4	2
2÷ 4	3− 8	5	7− 1	2	1− 7	6	4− 3
2	2− 6	4	8	1	15× 5	3	7
2÷ 1	2	1− 8	8+ 3	5	14× 6	11+ 7	4
2− 3	5	7	2− 4	6	8	2÷ 2	1
5− 8	3	1− 6	7	2÷ 4	2	4− 1	5

88

2÷ 6	3	14+ 7	5	2÷ 4	2	7− 1	8
4÷ 4	128× 8	2	2− 3	5	7 7	15+ 6	3÷ 1
1	2	8	15+ 7	2÷ 6	4	5	3
10× 2	1	5	8	3	168× 6	7	4
15+ 7	5	2÷ 3	6	8	7− 1	48× 4	2
3	24× 4	1	2− 2	8+ 7	120× 5	8	6
3− 8	17+ 7	6	4	1	3	48× 2	2− 5
5	6	4	1− 1	2	8	3	7

5− 6	**24×** 4	1	**3−** 8	5	**18+** 7	3	**5−** 2
1	2	3	**2÷** 4	**14+** 6	5	8	7
14+ 7	**4−** 1	5	2	3	**48×** 8	6	**60×** 4
3	**26+** 8	**42×** 6	1	**224×** 7	4	**56×** 2	5
4	5	**40×** 2	7	8	**10+** 6	1	3
3− 2	6	4	5	1	3	7	**2−** 8
5	7	**56×** 8	**1−** 3	2	**2÷** 1	4	6
5− 8	3	7	**24×** 6	4	2	**6+** 5	1

7− 1	**160×** 8	4	**3÷** 3	**2−** 5	**17+** 7	6	**3÷** 2
8	**10+** 2	5	1	3	4	**13+** 7	6
4− 7	1	**6−** 8	2	**18+** 4	6	5	**1−** 3
3	7	**6** 6	**26+** 5	**15+** 2	8	1	4
10+ 5	3	2	8	6	**24×** 1	**3−** 4	7
2− 2	**4÷** 4	1	6	7	3	8	**4−** 5
4	**2÷** 6	3	7	**16×** 8	**3−** 5	2	1
1− 6	5	**11+** 7	4	1	2	**5−** 3	8

91

168× 7	4	6	6+ 3	1	2	3− 5	14+ 8
6− 8	17+ 5	12× 1	4	3	4− 7	2	6
2	8	4	175× 7	5	3	1− 6	2÷ 1
6× 1	6	11+ 3	5	4− 8	4	7	2
7+ 5	2	8	24× 1	13+ 7	6	2÷ 4	2− 3
2÷ 3	10+ 7	2	6	4	4− 1	8	5
6	1	1− 7	8	192× 2	5	2− 3	11+ 4
60× 4	3	5	2	6	8	1	7

92

2÷ 8	4	2− 5	3÷ 2	16+ 1	7	2÷ 3	6
3− 2	5	7	6	80× 4	8	1− 1	4− 3
7+ 3	5− 6	7− 8	1	5	4	2	7
4	1	4− 3	7	5− 8	13+ 2	6	5
5− 1	4÷ 2	20× 4	5	3	336× 6	7	8
6	8	4÷ 1	4	12+ 7	3	9+ 5	1− 2
4− 7	3	3÷ 6	24× 8	2	30× 5	4	1
2− 5	7	2	3	6	1	2÷ 8	4

42×		3÷		21+	192×		
7	**6**	**1**	**3**	**5**	**4**	**8**	**2**
28×		13+	8+			3+	3−
4	**7**	**8**	**1**	**6**	**3**	**2**	**5**
12+							
3	**5**	**2**	**7**	**4**	**6**	**1**	**8**
6+			4÷		7−	13+	
5	**4**	**3**	**8**	**2**	**1**	**7**	**6**
	13+	168×	3−			20×	
1	**2**	**7**	**6**	**3**	**8**	**5**	**4**
			1−	5−		126×	
8	**3**	**4**	**5**	**7**	**2**	**6**	**1**
2÷				9+	19+		
2	**1**	**6**	**4**	**8**	**5**	**3**	**7**
2−		10×					
6	**8**	**5**	**2**	**1**	**7**	**4**	**3**

1−		1−		56×		7+	6−
5	**4**	**2**	**3**	**8**	**7**	**6**	**1**
30×		22+	1−		7−		
6	**5**	**4**	**2**	**3**	**8**	**1**	**7**
11+						4	13+
2	**3**	**7**	**6**	**5**	**1**	**4**	**8**
112×		13+	10+				
7	**6**	**8**	**4**	**1**	**2**	**3**	**5**
			5−		13+		2÷
8	**2**	**5**	**1**	**6**	**4**	**7**	**3**
9+		504×			15×		
1	**8**	**3**	**7**	**4**	**5**	**2**	**6**
4÷			1−			3−	2÷
4	**1**	**6**	**8**	**7**	**3**	**5**	**2**
4−		4−		4−			
3	**7**	**1**	**5**	**2**	**6**	**8**	**4**

95

336× 7	3	4	**4÷** 8	2	**5−** 6	1	**4−** 5
4	**21+** 6	**150×** 2	3	5	**15+** 8	7	1
1	7	**10+** 6	5	**24×** 8	3	**96×** 4	2
24+ 5	8	3	1	**4÷** 4	**14×** 7	2	6
8	4	**210×** 7	6	1	2	**2−** 5	3
288× 6	2	5	**168×** 4	**2−** 3	1	**1−** 8	7
2	5	1	7	6	**1−** 4	3	**2÷** 8
3	1	8	**5−** 2	7	**1−** 5	6	4

96

3+ 2	**21×** 7	**96×** 6	8	**108×** 4	9	3	**140×** 5	**6+** 1
1	3	2	**432×** 9	8	6	7	4	5
24+ 7	4	5	**162×** 3	**8−** 9	1	**3÷** 2	6	**11+** 8
24× 4	8	9	6	7	**15×** 3	5	1	2
6	**3÷** 2	**4÷** 4	**120×** 5	3	8	**8×** 1	**25+** 9	**7** 7
135× 3	6	1	**11+** 4	5	2	8	7	9
5	9	**10+** 7	**3+** 2	1	**19+** 4	6	**5−** 8	3
40× 8	5	3	**42×** 1	6	7	9	**2÷** 2	4
8− 9	1	**112×** 8	7	2	**1−** 5	4	**2÷** 3	6

97

63×1	7	9	**18+**4	6	8	**30×**2	3	5
5−3	8	**140×**5	7	4	**8−**9	1	**3÷**6	2
3+2	1	**48×**6	**17+**8	9	**35×**5	**13+**7	**12×**4	3
13+4	9	8	**13+**3	5	7	6	**1−**2	1
12+7	3	**8+**1	5	**5−**8	**24×**2	**36×**4	**270×**9	6
30×6	2	7	**3+**1	3	4	9	5	**17+**8
5	**10+**6	4	2	**6−**1	3	**1−**8	7	9
17+8	**10×**5	2	**15+**9	7	**18×**6	3	1	**28×**4
9	**12×**4	3	6	**3+**2	1	**3−**5	8	7

98

21×7	3	1	**24×**6	4	**315×**9	5	**4÷**8	**2−**2
8−1	**30×**5	3	**72×**8	9	6	7	2	4
9	2	**7**7	**11+**5	6	8	**12+**4	**10+**3	**8−**1
66	**17+**8	5	4	**9+**1	3	2	7	9
2÷4	**8−**9	**6−**8	2	3	**3+**1	6	**2−**5	7
8	1	**1−**6	7	5	2	**17+**9	**24×**4	**8+**3
15×3	**5−**4	9	**3+**1	2	**3−**7	8	6	5
5	**9+**7	2	**24×**3	8	4	**15×**1	**8−**9	**48×**6
48×2	6	4	**16+**9	7	5	3	1	8

99

2÷ 3	6	21+ 5	3+ 2	1	28× 4	7	1− 8	9
2÷ 4	1− 8	6	3	7	8− 9	1	45× 5	5+ 2
2	7	3+ 1	18+ 6	4	8	40× 5	9	3
432× 9	2÷ 1	2	3− 4	13+ 6	7	8	7+ 3	140× 5
6	2	735× 3	1	17+ 8	5 5	54× 9	4	7
8	3÷ 3	7	5	9	1	2	3÷ 6	4
35× 1	9	720× 4	7	5 5	3	126× 6	2	15+ 8
5	4	9	576× 8	3÷ 2	6	3	7	1
7	5	8	9	9+ 3	2	4	1	6

100

18+ 6	3+ 2	1	45× 9	5	10+ 3	7	11+ 4	2− 8
3	5	4	1	17+ 9	8	7− 2	7	6
35× 5	17+ 8	224× 7	4	3÷ 6	2	9	2÷ 1	6− 3
7	3	8	9+ 5	4	336× 6	1	2	9
4 4	6	24× 3	8	3+ 1	7	90× 5	9	2
8− 9	3− 4	2÷ 6	3	2	1	8	1400× 5	7
1	7	3÷ 2	6	3÷ 3	9	1− 4	8	5
6− 2	8− 1	9	98× 7	3− 8	5	3	2÷ 6	4÷ 4
8	4− 9	5	2	7	2− 4	6	3	1

101

9 (3÷)	2 (2÷)	4	6 (1−)	5	3 (21×)	7	1	8 (40×)
3	1 (6−)	7	4 (2÷)	8	9 (5−)	2 (3÷)	6	5
7 (1−)	8 (2÷)	9 (8−)	3 (2÷)	6	4	5 (3−)	2 (7+)	1 (3÷)
6	4	1	2 (18+)	9	7	8	5	3
1 (3+)	3 (90×)	6	7 (16+)	4	5	9 (17+)	8	2 (3÷)
2	5	3 (3÷)	1	7 (1−)	8	4 (36×)	9	6
5 (2−)	7	2 (3−)	8 (48×)	1	6	3 (3÷)	4 (5−)	9
8 (192×)	6	5	9 (9)	3 (5+)	2	1	7 (196×)	4
4	9 (17+)	8	5 (10×)	2	1	6 (2÷)	3	7

102

2 (3+)	3 (2÷)	1 (42×)	7	6	4 (3−)	5 (360×)	9	8
1	6	8 (2÷)	4	3 (4−)	7	9 (5−)	2 (6−)	5 (6+)
6 (13+)	5 (2−)	3 (3÷)	9	7	2 (3+)	4	8	1
3	7	9 (45×)	5	8 (17+)	1	6 (18×)	4 (2÷)	2
4	8 (13+)	5	2 (3+)	9	6 (17+)	1	3 (4−)	7
7 (12+)	9 (8−)	4 (4)	1	2 (7+)	8	3	5 (30×)	6
5	1	2 (3÷)	6	4	3	8 (6−)	7 (42×)	9 (3÷)
9 (1−)	4 (2÷)	7 (15+)	8	1	5 (4−)	2	6	3
8	2	6 (90×)	3	5	9	7 (28×)	1	4

103

3÷		35×		8−		28+	10+	
6	**2**	**5**	**7**	**1**	**9**	**8**	**4**	**3**
8+	23+	3÷						19+
1	**9**	**2**	**6**	**8**	**5**	**7**	**3**	**4**
			135×			3+		
4	**6**	**8**	**5**	**9**	**3**	**2**	**1**	**7**
	144×		3+	30×	6−	11+		
3	**4**	**9**	**1**	**5**	**7**	**6**	**2**	**8**
35×	18+						270×	8−
7	**8**	**4**	**2**	**6**	**1**	**3**	**5**	**9**
		7	17+	24×	3÷	20×		
5	**3**	**7**	**8**	**2**	**6**	**4**	**9**	**1**
17+		2÷						60×
8	**7**	**3**	**9**	**4**	**2**	**1**	**6**	**5**
	7+		84×		4−		504×	
9	**1**	**6**	**4**	**3**	**8**	**5**	**7**	**2**
2								
2	**5**	**1**	**3**	**7**	**4**	**9**	**8**	**6**

104

2÷	16×		4−		23+	14+		8−
6	**1**	**8**	**7**	**3**	**4**	**2**	**5**	**9**
	12+		8−	3−		6		
3	**5**	**2**	**9**	**4**	**8**	**6**	**7**	**1**
14+							168×	
9	**2**	**5**	**1**	**7**	**3**	**8**	**4**	**6**
	126×		2÷		3+		17+	
5	**6**	**3**	**4**	**8**	**2**	**1**	**9**	**7**
4÷			810×					2
1	**4**	**7**	**5**	**6**	**9**	**3**	**8**	**2**
11+	8−		7+		42×		720×	
4	**9**	**1**	**2**	**5**	**6**	**7**	**3**	**8**
	84×		2−	3+	8−			
7	**3**	**4**	**8**	**2**	**1**	**9**	**6**	**5**
128×		15+			140×		8+	12×
8	**7**	**9**	**6**	**1**	**5**	**4**	**2**	**3**
			6−					
2	**8**	**6**	**3**	**9**	**7**	**5**	**1**	**4**

105

[50×]2	5	[16×]8	[3÷]1	[2÷]3	6	[36×]4	9	[17+]7
5	1	2	3	[1−]8	7	[17+]9	4	6
[63×]9	[1−]3	[35×]7	5	[4÷]4	1	8	[3÷]6	2
7	2	[8−]1	9	[14+]5	[23+]4	6	[5−]3	8
[54×]6	9	[3]3	7	2	5	[3+]1	[2÷]8	4
[3÷]1	[28×]7	[5−]9	4	[6]6	8	2	[2−]5	3
3	4	[14+]6	8	[7−]9	2	[8+]5	[8+]7	1
[8]8	[15+]6	4	[4−]2	[2−]7	9	3	[15+]1	5
[2÷]4	8	5	6	[3÷]1	3	[5−]7	2	9

106

[13+]3	[8−]1	9	[3÷]2	6	[4−]4	8	[35×]5	7
4	6	[14+]8	3	[4−]5	9	[210×]7	[5−]2	[4÷]1
[6×]1	2	3	[17+]8	9	5	6	7	4
[40×]5	3	[14+]1	[24×]4	[42×]2	7	[17+]9	8	[6]6
2	4	7	6	[8]8	3	[8−]1	9	[3−]5
[42×]7	[17+]9	6	1	[2÷]4	8	[8+]5	3	2
6	8	[13+]2	[105×]5	7	[6+]1	3	[4÷]4	[17+]9
[360×]9	5	4	7	3	[48×]6	2	1	8
8	[2−]7	5	[8−]9	1	2	4	[2÷]6	3

107

4÷ 8	756× 3	2	315× 9	7	5	4÷ 1	4	19+ 6
2	6	3	7	8− 1	15+ 4	8	16+ 9	5
20× 4	1	13+ 7	6	9	3	5	2	8
270× 6	5	5− 9	4	144× 8	5+ 2	3	8+ 1	7
9	112× 2	2÷ 4	8	3	7 7	12+ 6	5	1
5	7	4÷ 8	2	6	8− 1	9	12× 3	4
11+ 3	8	5− 6	1	100× 5	108× 9	19+ 4	7	6× 2
7	8− 9	1	5	4	6	2	8	3
1	9+ 4	5	48× 3	2	8	22+ 7	6	9

108

3÷ 3	9	1− 2	168× 6	7	30× 5	8+ 1	2÷ 8	4
20× 1	4÷ 8	3	4	8− 9	6	7	50× 2	5
4	2	2÷ 6	3	1	2− 7	9	5	1− 8
5	8− 1	9	3+ 2	128× 4	8	2÷ 6	3	7
18× 2	21× 7	2− 5	1	8 8	4	7+ 3	3− 9	7+ 6
9	3	7	16+ 8	5	18× 2	4	6	1
2− 6	4	7− 8	7 7	3	9	3− 5	2÷ 1	2
13+ 7	6	1	30× 5	2	3	8	36× 4	9
3− 8	5	19+ 4	9	6	3+ 1	2	10+ 7	3

109

8 ₁₈₊	**9** _{36×}	**4**	**2** ₉₊	**5** ₁₃₊	**1** _{8−}	**3** _{2÷}	**6**	**7** ₁₁₊
3	**7**	**6**	**1**	**8**	**9**	**2** ₁₇₊	**5** ₈₊	**4**
2 _{112×}	**6** ₁₉₊	**9**	**4**	**1** ₇₊	**7**	**8**	**3**	**5** _{1−}
7	**8**	**3** _{168×}	**5** ₅	**2**	**4**	**9** _{8−}	**1**	**6**
5 _{2−}	**3**	**8**	**9** ₁₇₊	**6** ₆	**2** _{2÷}	**4**	**7** _{6−}	**1**
1 _{16×}	**4**	**7**	**8**	**3** _{135×}	**5**	**6** _{54×}	**9**	**2** _{4÷}
4	**1** _{15×}	**5**	**3**	**9**	**6** _{1008×}	**7**	**2** _{4÷}	**8**
6 ₂₀₊	**5**	**2** _{84×}	**7**	**4** _{28×}	**3**	**1**	**8**	**9** _{6−}
9	**2** _{2÷}	**1**	**6**	**7**	**8**	**5** ₉₊	**4**	**3**

110

1 _{72×}	**3**	**2** _{3−}	**5**	**7** _{210×}	**6**	**4** _{2÷}	**8**	**9** _{27×}
4	**6**	**9** _{8−}	**2** ₁₈₊	**5**	**8** ₁₅₊	**7**	**3**	**1**
6 _{48×}	**8**	**1**	**7**	**9**	**4** _{5−}	**2** _{30×}	**5**	**3**
5 ₁₇₊	**2** ₃₊	**3** _{5−}	**1** _{8−}	**4** ₇₊	**9**	**8** _{240×}	**7** _{1−}	**6**
2	**1**	**8**	**9**	**3**	**5** ₅	**6**	**4** ₁₁₊	**7**
3	**7**	**6** _{48×}	**8**	**2** ₂	**1** ₃₊	**5**	**9** _{5−}	**4**
7 ₁₁₊	**4**	**5** _{20×}	**3** ₁₈₊	**1**	**2**	**9** ₂₃₊	**6**	**8**
9 _{4−}	**5**	**4**	**6**	**8** ₂₀₊	**7** _{4−}	**3**	**1** _{10×}	**2**
8 ₁₇₊	**9**	**7** _{3−}	**4**	**6**	**3**	**1**	**2**	**5**

111

12× 3	4	112× 2	12+ 5	6	1	45360× 9	7	8
40× 4	2	7	8	3	6	5	8− 9	1
5	15+ 6	8	1	8− 9	12× 4	3	9+ 2	7
17+ 8	9	13+ 6	7	1	6× 3	2	1− 4	5
63× 7	2− 5	3÷ 3	9	1− 4	3+ 2	1	24× 8	3÷ 6
9	7	16× 1	4	5	2688× 8	6	3	2
3+ 1	3÷ 3	4	3÷ 6	2	7	8	30× 5	13+ 9
2	1	158760× 9	120× 3	8	5	7	6	4
2− 6	8	5	2	7	9	4	2− 1	3

112

6 6	6× 1	315× 7	40× 2	5	4	90× 3	16+ 9	24+ 8
4÷ 4	2	5	30+ 8	7	1	6	3	9
1	3	9	6	54× 2	8	5	4	7
1− 9	20× 5	4	420× 7	3	378× 6	6− 8	2	2÷ 1
8	288× 6	3	5	9	7	140× 4	1	2
2	8	2− 6	3	4	9	3+ 1	7	5
11+ 7	4	8	8− 9	1	450× 5	2	2÷ 6	3
135× 3	20+ 7	1	4	8	2	9	5	192× 6
5	9	2÷ 2	1	126× 6	3	7	8	4

113

25× **1**	24× **6**	**4**	8+ **3**	24+ **7**	**8**	**9**	7− **2**
5	19+ **1**	1440× **8**	2− **7**	**2**	**3**	3÷ **6**	4 **4**	**9**

25× **1**	24× **6**	**4**	8+ **3**	24+ **7**	**8**	**9**	7− **2**
5	19+ **1**	1440× **8**	2− **7**	**2**	**3**	3÷ **6**	4 **4**	**9**
3	**8**	**9**	**5**	3− **7**	**4**	**2**	6+ **1**	5− **6**
7	**4**	**5**	17+ **8**	8− **9**	108× **6**	21× **3**	**2**	**1**
4÷ **8**	5− **9**	**4**	**6**	**1**	**2**	**7**	**3**	5 **5**
2	252× **6**	**7**	**3**	120× **4**	**9**	**1**	3− **5**	56× **8**
2÷ **4**	**2**	**3**	8− **1**	**6**	**5**	21+ **9**	**8**	**7**
378× **6**	3 **3**	**2**	**9**	14+ **8**	**1**	**5**	**7**	7+ **4**
9	**7**	2÷ **1**	**2**	**5**	18+ **8**	**4**	**6**	**3**

114

4÷ **1**	**4**	80× **2**	**5**	3− **9**	17+ **3**	**7**	48× **6**	**8**
14+ **4**	2÷ **2**	3÷ **9**	**8**	**6**	**7**	7+ **5**	12× **3**	8− **1**
7	**1**	**3**	240× **6**	**8**	**5**	**2**	**4**	**9**
3	1− **8**	**7**	15+ **4**	1 **1**	8− **9**	13+ **6**	**5**	**2**
45× **5**	2− **7**	2÷ **4**	**9**	**2**	**1**	3÷ **3**	4÷ **8**	10+ **6**
9	**5**	**8**	16+ **7**	**3**	**6**	**1**	**2**	**4**
4÷ **2**	2÷ **6**	6× **1**	**3**	2− **5**	16+ **8**	**4**	8− **9**	7 **7**
8	**3**	1− **6**	**2**	**7**	**4**	72× **9**	**1**	105× **5**
3− **6**	**9**	**5**	8× **1**	**4**	**2**	**8**	**7**	**3**

115

168× 7	6	4	3÷ 3	1	5	13+ 2	144× 9	8
4÷ 4	2÷ 1	4÷ 2	8	9 9	3	5	42× 6	2− 7
1	2	30+ 8	4	6	9	3	7	5
2÷ 8	4	42× 1	5− 2	4− 7	48× 6	8− 9	15× 5	3
15× 5	4− 9	6	7	3	8	1	2÷ 4	7− 2
3	5	7	7+ 1	2	4	6 6	8	9
4− 2	4− 3	270× 9	6	1120× 5	7	8	3÷ 1	4÷ 4
6	7	5	19+ 9	8	2	4	3	1
17+ 9	8	12+ 3	5	4	8+ 1	7	3÷ 2	6

116

5− 9	1− 5	28× 7	4	90× 3	6− 2	8	2− 6	8− 1
4	6	7− 1	2	5	3	2− 7	8	9
42× 7	13+ 4	8	8− 9	1	60× 6	5	3÷ 3	1− 2
6	9	2÷ 4	8	56× 7	5	2	1	3
3+ 1	6− 7	10× 2	4− 3	8	17+ 9	12× 4	4− 5	2− 6
2	1	5	7	54× 6	8	3	9	4
360× 5	8	3	11+ 6	9	3− 4	18+ 1	2	7
3	7− 2	9	5	4 4	1	42× 6	7	8
8 8	2÷ 3	6	10+ 1	2	7	18+ 9	4	5

117

2÷ 2	4	8− 1	9	11+ 7	10× 5	2− 6	8	3÷ 3
45× 5	96× 8	3− 4	3	1	2	4− 7	2− 6	9
9	2	7	2÷ 8	11+ 5	6	3	4	17+ 1
4÷ 1	6	17+ 8	4	1− 2	3	15+ 5	9	7
4	7 7	9	2− 5	3	1	8	3÷ 2	6
945× 7	3	11+ 6	14× 2	5− 4	9	1	200× 5	8
2÷ 3	9	2	7	2− 6	8	36× 4	8+ 1	5
6	5	3	18+ 1	8	11+ 4	9	7	2÷ 2
7− 8	1	30× 5	6	9	7	6× 2	3	4

118

192× 4	6	8	7+ 5	2	6− 1	7	16+ 3	9
90× 3	13+ 9	5− 2	7	6+ 1	5	2− 8	6	4
6	4	24+ 7	8	9	4− 2	6+ 1	5	6× 3
5	1− 8	9	1− 3	4	6	60× 2	24+ 7	1
8− 1	126× 7	3	6	2÷ 8	4	5	9	2
9	4÷ 1	4	5− 2	7	6− 3	6	8	13+ 5
5− 7	2− 3	12+ 6	1	5	9	2÷ 4	2	8
2	5	36× 1	9	48× 6	8	1− 3	4	42× 7
80× 8	2	5	4	19+ 3	7	9	1	6

119

^{3−}2	^{2−}5	3	^{2÷}8	4	^{252×}6	^{288×}9	⁸⁺7	1
5	^{12×}1	¹⁰⁺6	¹⁶⁺7	2	3	4	8	¹⁷⁺9
^{8−}1	2	4	9	^{48×}6	7	^{75×}5	3	8
9	6	¹¹⁺2	4	1	³⁰⁺8	3	5	^{105×}7
⁷7	^{8−}9	1	5	8	4	^{3÷}2	6	3
^{2−}4	¹⁸⁺7	^{8×}8	1	²⁶⁺3	9	6	¹²⁺2	5
6	8	^{2−}7	3	5	³⁺2	1	9	^{2÷}4
¹¹⁺8	3	5	6	9	1	^{1120×}7	4	2
3	¹³⁺4	9	⁹⁺2	7	5	8	^{5−}1	6

120

^{4÷}2	8	^{10×}5	^{8−}1	9	^{2−}4	6	^{4−}7	3
⁶⁺5	1	2	^{168×}6	^{3÷}3	9	¹⁹⁺7	4	8
1	^{3÷}2	6	4	7	^{24×}8	3	^{7−}9	²³⁺5
^{2−}6	^{756×}4	^{8−}1	9	^{24×}8	3	¹⁸⁺5	2	7
8	3	^{2÷}4	2	^{6−}1	7	9	⁵5	6
7	9	^{3−}8	5	^{3÷}6	2	4	^{2÷}3	1
^{1−}3	^{4−}5	9	¹⁷⁺7	2	^{7−}1	8	6	4
4	¹⁷⁺7	3	8	^{1−}5	6	²2	^{8−}1	9
^{54×}9	6	7	^{12×}3	4	⁶⁺5	1	^{4÷}8	2

121

21× 7	17+ 2	96× 4	3	8	8− 1	9	11+ 5	6
3	6	9	14+ 8	60× 4	5	8+ 1	7	3+ 2
48× 8	36× 4	3+ 2	6	3	21+ 7	5	9	1
6	9	1	13+ 7	4− 2	19+ 4	8	18× 3	17+ 5
3+ 2	7 7	280× 5	4	6	17+ 8	3	1	9
1	10+ 5	8	2	7 7	9	4	6	3
4	1	7	8− 9	810× 5	3	3÷ 6	2	1− 8
4− 5	72× 8	3	1	9	6	2÷ 2	4	7
9	3	12+ 6	5	1	5− 2	7	4− 8	4

122

54× 9	6	3− 8	8− 1	1− 7	14+ 2	3	4	5
4− 3	7	5	9	6	3÷ 1	14+ 4	8	2÷ 2
192× 4	8	63× 9	7	28+ 5	3	3÷ 6	2	1
6	105× 3	7	5	4	8	2	1134× 1	9
40× 8	5	2− 6	4	2 2	7	8− 1	9	3
16+ 5	6+ 2	1	3	7− 8	4	1− 9	6	7
7	4	1− 3	2	1	20+ 9	8	175× 5	10+ 6
8− 1	9	2− 2	48× 8	3÷ 3	6	5	7	4
1− 2	1	4	6	9	5	168× 7	3	8

123

540×5	2	9	6	16+4	1	7−8	84×3	7
3 3	160×5	8	9	2	240×6	1	2−7	4
4÷2	4	1	168×7	6	8	5	9	15×3
8	108×6	210×5	4	4−7	3	216×9	64×2	1
6	3	7	8−1	9	4	2	8	5
63×7	1	6	13+5	6−8	2	3	4	17+9
1	9+7	2	3	5	18+9	4	252×6	8
9	2÷8	4	13+2	3	5	7	1	13+6
24+4	9	3	8	1	7	6	5	2

124

120×5	4	6	2÷1	2	21+3	7	336×8	8−9
3÷3	48×8	3−5	17+4	6	2	9	7	1
9	6	8	2160×5	7	16+1	4	2	3
192×6	4−3	7	8	15+9	4	6+1	5	14+2
8	7−9	2	3	5	7	6 6	1	4
4	1−2	3	9	1	200×5	14+8	6	7
14×7	6+1	8−9	2	14+3	8	5	22+4	6
2	5	1	7	4	11+6	3	9	3−8
28×1	7	4	48×6	8	9 9	2	3	5

125

3+ 2	1− 6	1− 3	4	72× 9	8	36× 1	11+ 7	11+ 5
1	7	5 5	17+ 8	12+ 2	3	9	4	6
2− 5	3+ 2	1	9	5− 6	7	4	2− 8	5− 3
3	15+ 4	10× 2	5	1	27+ 9	7	6	8
2÷ 8	1	7	2− 6	4	3+ 2	5	3÷ 3	9
4	3	56× 8	7	2− 5	1	6	45× 9	3+ 2
30+ 9	8	4	5+ 3	7	384× 6	2	5	1
42× 6	4− 5	9	2	8	4	5− 3	1− 1	3− 7
7	9	5− 6	1	2− 3	5	8	2	4

126

48× 6	2	315× 7	5	8− 9	1	8× 8	84× 3	4
21× 3	4	9	24+ 8	48× 6	90× 5	1	7	6× 2
7	11+ 5	2÷ 2	9	8	6	5− 4	3+ 1	3
7− 8	6	4	7	14+ 1	3	9	2	13+ 5
1	120× 3	5	2	7	4	108× 6	9	8
2− 5	7	8	4÷ 4	1− 3	2− 9	2	7+ 6	1
23+ 4	8	18× 6	1	2	7	16+ 3	1890× 5	9
9	1	3	162× 6	1− 4	21+ 2	5	8	7
2	9	1	3	5	8	7	4	6

127

20×1	3÷6	2	⁷7	3÷9	14+4	16+8	5	3
5	2−7	3+1	2	3	6	4	4÷8	8−9
4	5	378×6	9	7	11+8	3	2	1
2÷8	4	2−7	90×6	5	3	8−9	64×1	2
3÷3	8−9	5	96×8	6	2	1	1−7	4
9	1	6−3	17+4	2	5	1−7	6	8
4÷2	8	9	5	2÷4	1	6	4−3	7
1−6	12×3	4	1	8	18+7	2	9	1−5
7	4÷2	8	13+3	1	9	1−5	4	6

128

5−9	4−7	3	3+1	2	30×5	6	2÷8	4
4	4−5	24+8	2	4÷1	4−3	7	3−6	9
18+7	9	6	8	4	10×2	1	5	2÷3
3	8	27+7	9	6+5	1	2÷2	4	6
3−5	2	4	21+7	8	6	³3	8−9	1
17+6	3	2	5	2−9	7	3−4	1	4÷8
8	2−4	6×1	6	4−7	135×9	5	3	2
2÷1	6	1−5	4	3	17+8	9	14×2	7
2	8−1	9	2÷3	6	4−4	8	2−7	5

129

4− 1	4− 3	7	12+ 4	16× 8	20+ 5	6	9	7− 2
5	1− 4	3	8	1	2	1− 7	6	9
2÷ 4	2	8− 1	9	1− 7	8	14+ 5	3	6
17+ 8	1440× 6	40× 5	15+ 7	4 4	21× 3	8− 9	2÷ 2	4− 1
9	8	2	6	3÷ 3	7	1	4	5
6	5	4	2	9	1	16+ 8	4− 7	3
9+ 2	7	3− 8	5	3− 6	9	3	1	4
4− 7	8− 1	9	3÷ 3	13+ 2	6	1− 4	5	1− 8
3	54× 9	6	1	5	14+ 4	2	8	7

130

72× 6	840× 5	2	3	7	4	8− 1	9	23+ 8
4	3	17+ 8	35× 5	7− 1	2400× 2	1− 7	6	9
12+ 3	18+ 2	9	7	8	5	6	24× 1	10+ 4
7	9	2− 4	6	5	8	16+ 2	3	1
2	7	6	224× 1	28+ 4	8− 9	3	8	5
3− 5	8	7	4	6	1	9	2	2÷ 3
8	18+ 1	3	2	9	7	1− 5	4	6
8− 1	24× 4	5	9	144× 3	6	8	2− 7	5− 2
9	6	1	48× 8	2	3	4 4	5	7

131

26+ 7	9	12× 4	14+ 8	6	4- 1	5	5+ 3	2
4	6	3	18+ 9	2	40× 5	15+ 8	7	8- 1
2÷ 1	2	1- 5	6	7	8	12× 3	4	9
3 3	23+ 7	8- 9	1	14+ 4	48× 2	14+ 6	8	15× 5
8	5	96× 6	7 7	9	4	2÷ 1	2	3
360× 5	3	8	2	1	6	36× 4	9	336× 7
9	4	3÷ 1	3	17+ 8	21× 7	3- 2	5	6
2	48× 1	5- 7	4	5	3	15+ 9	6	8
6	8	2	2- 5	3	2- 9	7	4÷ 1	4

132

30× 5	6	22+ 2	9	3	7	1	896× 4	8
4- 3	72× 9	24× 6	4	240× 8	5	2	2÷ 1	7
7	8	1	27+ 6	4- 5	21+ 9	3	2	4
2÷ 6	3	5	7	9	1	4	4÷ 8	2
3- 8	5	9	8× 1	2	4	7	2÷ 6	3
15+ 2	1	3	5	4	3024× 8	9	7	6
192× 4	2	8	3	1260× 7	6	5	10+ 9	1
8- 9	112× 7	4	112× 8	1	5+ 2	2÷ 6	3	19+ 5
1	4	7	2	6	3	8 8	5	9

133

18+ 9	3÷ 2	6	1− 8	7	60× 4	3	5	6+ 1
1	36× 9	4	1− 7	72× 6	3	4÷ 2	8	5
8	3− 5	7− 2	6	4	6− 1	7	189× 9	3
168× 6	8	9	10+ 3	45× 5	17+ 2	13+ 4	1	7
7	2− 3	5	2	1	9	8	18+ 6	4 4
4	3− 7	9+ 8	5	9	6	1	3	2
2 2	4	1	8− 9	48× 3	1− 5	6	7	23+ 8
2− 3	1− 6	7	1	2	8	9+ 5	4	9
5	3÷ 1	3	2÷ 4	8	126× 7	9	2	6

134

1− 2	2÷ 4	8	8− 9	72× 3	30× 1	5	6	2− 7
3	20+ 5	5− 2	1	4	6	18+ 8	7	9
6	9	7	10+ 4	3− 5	504× 8	1	3	2÷ 2
3− 5	2	19+ 9	6	8	30× 3	7	8× 4	1
24× 8	3	4	1− 7	6	2	9	1	5 5
8+ 1	7	6	2− 3	8− 9	5	10+ 4	2	48× 8
336× 7	8	3÷ 3	5	1	4	2	17+ 9	6
36× 9	6	1	4÷ 8	882× 2	7	3	5	7+ 4
4	6+ 1	5	2	7	9	2− 6	8	3

135

18× 1	6	**12+** 2	7	3	**72×** 8	9	**15+** 4	5
3	**8−** 1	9	**96×** 4	**35×** 7	**16+** 5	**4÷** 8	2	6
21+ 8	3	4	6	5	9	2	**252×** 7	**1** 1
2	8	**2−** 3	5	1	**13+** 7	6	9	4
100× 5	**504×** 9	7	8	**7−** 2	**24×** 4	1	6	**10+** 3
4	5	**7−** 8	**1−** 2	9	**4−** 6	**4−** 3	**14+** 1	7
378× 9	**2÷** 4	1	3	**6** 6	2	7	5	**144×** 8
7	2	**1−** 6	**8−** 1	**2÷** 4	**3÷** 3	**12+** 5	8	9
6	**7** 7	5	9	8	1	4	3	2

136

1− 5	**30+** 7	8	6	9	**2÷** 4	2	**3÷** 1	3
4	**1890×** 5	3	7	**2** 2	**34+** 6	8	**54×** 9	**8+** 1
9	2	5	8	4	3	1	6	7
6 6	**8−** 1	9	**18+** 4	**30×** 5	**24+** 8	**588×** 7	**1440×** 3	2
2÷ 1	**6×** 3	2	5	6	9	4	7	8
2	**2÷** 8	4	9	1	7	3	5	6
22+ 7	6	**6+** 1	2	3	**21+** 5	**288×** 9	8	**1−** 4
5− 3	9	**6−** 7	1	8	2	6	4	5
8	**504×** 4	6	3	7	**6+** 1	5	**7−** 2	9

137

6 6	8− 1	9	5− 2	20× 4	5	6− 3	1344× 8	7
360× 3	5	8	7	5− 1	14× 2	9	4	6
9+ 8	3	12+ 1	9	6	7	1− 4	5	15+ 2
1	30+ 7	2	15× 3	5	48× 6	8	9	4
15+ 2	8	6 6	2− 5	7	4÷ 4	1	3÷ 3	9
9	6	2− 5	12× 4	3	8	7	8+ 2	1
4	9	7	48× 1	1− 8	3÷ 3	4− 2	6	5
40× 5	2	4	8	9	1	1− 6	21× 7	3
14+ 7	4	3	6	18× 2	9	5	1	8 8

138

11+ 2	4	42× 6	7	8− 1	9	2− 5	168× 8	3
5	7− 2	12+ 8	1	5− 9	4	3	7	18+ 6
5184× 4	9	3	270× 6	4÷ 8	3− 5	2	1	7
8	24× 1	5	9	2	84× 6	4− 7	3	4
6	3	2÷ 1	3− 4	7	2	1− 8	9	5 5
3	8	2	15× 5	9+ 4	7	54× 9	6	20+ 1
9	13+ 6	56× 7	3	5	4÷ 1	4	2	8
35× 1	7	4	2	5− 3	8	240× 6	5	9
7	5	1− 9	8	2÷ 6	3	1	4	2

139

4− 1	5	189× 9	7	3	192× 4	8	13+ 6	2
384× 4	3÷ 3	4÷ 2	8	8− 9	1	6	5	105× 7
8	9	25+ 4	6× 1	6	9+ 7	2	3	5
6	192× 4	3	5	16× 8	2	1	126× 7	36× 9
2	8	6	7+ 3	1	2− 5	7	9	4
2− 3	6	5	4	24+ 7	8	9	2	1
5	10+ 1	7	4− 6	2	3÷ 9	3	18+ 4	8
7	2	72× 8	9	1− 4	3	600× 5	24× 1	6
2− 9	7	1− 1	2	5	6	4	8	3

140

3+ 2	1	17+ 6	17+ 8	5	3	288× 9	4	63× 7
2− 3	9+ 2	7	4	1	8+ 5	6 6	8	9
5	7	2− 8	6	12× 4	1	2	180× 9	1− 3
336× 8	42× 6	1	7	3	21+ 9	4	5	2
6	2− 5	3	8− 1	9	4	18+ 7	4÷ 2	8
7	72× 4	9	2	3÷ 6	8	1	3	4− 5
5− 4	11+ 3	4− 5	9	2	16+ 6	8	7	1
9	8	24× 4	3	392× 7	2	15+ 5	1	10+ 6
8− 1	9	2	5 5	8	7	3	6	4

141

3456× 8	2÷ 2	4	540× 3	9	5	80× 1	22+ 7	6
3	6	8+ 2	5	1	4	8	9	4− 7
6	4	24+ 9	7	8	2	5	10+ 1	3
2− 5	3	112× 8	2	7	54× 9	6	4	11+ 1
30+ 9	7	6	8	4− 5	1	84× 4	3	2
10+ 1	9	30× 5	24× 6	4	7	3	2	8
13+ 7	5	3	1	2	1008× 8	9	2160× 6	20× 4
2÷ 4	1	16+ 7	36× 9	3 3	15+ 6	2	8	5
2	8	1	4	6	3	7	5	9

142

6+ 5	180× 3	6	252× 9	4	7	14+ 2	8	8× 1
1	2	5	126× 3	7	6	4	9 9	8
10+ 2	1	3	4	4÷ 8	27+ 9	7	6	5
24+ 8	13+ 6	7	9+ 1	2	17+ 4	4− 9	5	10+ 3
9	7	2	6	10+ 1	8	5	3	4
5− 3	8	20× 4	5	9	2÷ 2	1	42× 7	6
17+ 7	1− 5	1296× 9	8	3	1	6	2÷ 4	126× 2
6	4	8+ 1	7	120× 5	3	8	2	9
4	1− 9	8	60× 2	6	5	2− 3	1	7

143

2− 1	3	360× 9	8	5	3− 4	7	3÷ 2	6
12+ 5	4	3	14+ 6	1	7	19+ 8	9	2
25+ 8	2	2− 5	3	17+ 7	6	4	56× 1	9 9
9	6	15+ 2	5	4	3	1	7	8
72× 6	72× 9	8	3− 4	3 3	2÷ 1	10× 2	5	13+ 7
4	2− 8	6	7	144× 9	2	2− 5	3	1
3	6− 1	7	8− 9	2	28+ 8	10+ 6	4	5
5− 2	28× 7	4	1	8	5	9	6	7+ 3
7	4− 5	1	108× 2	6	9	11+ 3	8	4

144

6+ 5	1	252× 7	4	9	3÷ 2	6	20+ 8	3
10+ 4	3	560× 5	2	30+ 6	7	8	9	1
3	9 9	1	7	8	1− 5	4	2	6
224× 7	54× 6	9	32× 1	4	8	6× 2	3	8+ 5
8	4	84× 3	35× 5	7	6 6	28+ 9	1	2
1	7	4	54× 9	2	3	5	6	8
108× 2	40× 5	8	23+ 6	3	27× 9	3− 1	4	20+ 7
9	96× 2	6	8	20× 5	1	3	19+ 7	4
6	8	2	3	1	4	7	5	9

³⁄÷ 1	3	²⁵²× 7	²¹⁶× 9	8	²⁴⁺ 5	2	⁴⁸× 6	4
²⁸⁰× 5	1	4	3	¹⁻ 6	7	9	8	2
8	7	9	²³⁺ 2	5	4	²÷ 6	⁹⁺ 1	3
¹²⁺ 6	²⁰× 4	5	7	⁷⁻ 1	8	3	2	³⁵⁺ 9
4	³÷ 6	2	5	⁸⁻ 9	1	⁷ 7	3	8
2	³⁻ 9	6	²⁸⁸× 8	¹²× 4	3	⁷⁻ 1	¹¹⁺ 7	5
³¹⁵× 9	5	²⁴× 1	6	3	2	8	4	7
7	⁸ 8	3	²⁸× 1	⁷⁻ 2	9	²⁰⁺ 4	5	6
⁶× 3	2	8	4	7	6	5	⁸⁻ 9	1

²¹⁶× 9	3	⁶⁻ 7	⁵⁻ 2	⁷⁺ 6	1	⁴⁻ 5	²⁰⁺ 8	4
4	2	1	7	¹⁻ 5	6	9	¹⁵⁺ 3	8
¹⁹⁺ 6	⁷⁻ 9	2	⁸⁺ 1	7	²⁴× 8	3	4	¹⁻ 5
3	4	²¹⁶× 8	⁸⁻ 9	1	¹²⁺ 2	¹⁷⁺ 7	5	6
⁵ 5	6	3	¹⁻ 8	9	7	4	2	¹¹⁺ 1
⁸⁰× 8	5	9	²÷ 4	2	3	6	1	7
2	³⁻ 8	5	²⁴× 6	4	¹⁰⁺ 9	1	¹⁻ 7	3
⁴⁹× 7	¹ 1	²⁴× 4	²⁻ 3	⁴⁰× 8	5	⁴÷ 2	6	¹⁶²× 9
1	7	6	5	¹⁻ 3	4	8	9	2

147

²¹⁶ˣ 9	6	4	⁸⁻ 1	¹⁵⁺ 7	2	¹²⁰ˣ 8	5	3
³⁻ 4	⁶ˣ 1	2	9	¹⁷⁺ 5	6	⁵⁻ 7	¹²⁰ˣ 3	8
7	²⁵²ˣ 4	3	¹⁴⁺ 6	9	²÷ 8	2	⁸⁺ 1	5
³÷ 6	9	7	8	3	4	5	2	⁴÷ 1
2	²⁻ 3	²¹⁶⁰ˣ 5	⁵⁻ 7	²⁻ 6	⁸⁻ 9	⁶ˣ 1	²÷ 8	4
²⁻ 3	5	9	2	8	1	6	4	¹⁴ˣ 7
5	8	6	¹⁰⁺ 4	1	3	²⁻ 9	7	2
¹⁶⁺ 8	7	1	²⁴⁺ 3	2	5	³⁶ˣ 4	9	⁶ 6
²÷ 1	2	⁸ 8	5	4	7	¹⁸⁺ 3	6	9

148

⁴÷ 2	8	⁸⁴⁰ˣ 5	1	7	4	6	⁶⁻ 3	9
²÷ 3	6	²⁴⁺ 7	¹¹⁺ 2	³⁻ 1	²⁷⁰ˣ 5	²⁸ˣ 4	¹⁷⁺ 9	8
⁶⁺ 1	5	8	6	4	9	7	⁶ˣ 2	3
¹⁸⁺ 5	7	9	3	²⁴⁺ 2	6	1	¹⁶⁰ˣ 8	4
6	3	4	7	8	¹²⁺ 2	9	1	5
⁵⁻ 4	²÷ 2	³⁰⁺ 6	8	9	7	¹²⁺ 3	5	⁸⁺ 1
9	1	² 2	²¹⁺ 5	¹⁻ 6	³÷ 3	⁶⁴⁰ˣ 8	4	7
²⁴⁺ 8	9	⁸⁺ 3	4	5	1	2	²¹⁺ 7	6
7	4	1	9	3	8	5	6	2

149

4÷ 8	2− 5	3	5− 2	7	24× 1	6	4	18+ 9
2	17+ 4	24+ 9	7	8	20+ 5	1	3	6
5	8	16+ 1	9	4	7	3÷ 2	6	3
8− 9	6× 3	6	3− 5	2	23+ 8	840× 7	6− 1	16+ 4
1	2	288× 4	8	9	6	3	7	5
756× 3	1	84× 2	24× 4	6	9	8	5	7
4	9	7	6	6× 1	3	3− 5	2	7− 8
1− 6	7	120× 8	3	5	2	5− 4	9	1
7	1− 6	5	3÷ 1	3	5− 4	9	4÷ 8	2

150

40× 1	8	1260× 6	7	14+ 3	2	9	80× 4	5
5	3÷ 3	5− 8	6	3− 7	8− 9	6− 1	24× 2	4
144× 8	9	3	5	4	1	7	6	2
3	216× 6	9	4	144× 8	8+ 5	2	1	56× 7
6	6+ 1	2	3	9	1120× 7	4	5	8
11+ 4	5	1296× 1	9	2	6	8	10+ 7	3
2	224× 7	5 5	1	6	4	26+ 3	8	162× 9
16+ 7	2	4	112× 8	4− 5	16+ 3	6	9	1
9	4	7	2	1	8	5	3	6